Fly-Tying Materials

Fly-Tying Materials

THEIR PROCUREMENT, USE, AND PROTECTION

ERIC LEISER

Introduction by Art Flick

FULLY ILLUSTRATED

CROWN PUBLISHERS, INC., NEW YORK

Library of Congress Catalog Card Number: 72–96650

Printed in the United States of America

Published simultaneously in Canada by General Publishing Company Limited

Second Printing, April, 1974

Acknowledgments

First things first, and since this book would not have been written without the encouragement of my friends and companions, not to mention the many tiers who have requested some of the information contained herein, I can, at the very least, acknowledge and thank them for their contributions.

In the art of fly tying, I doubt if one of us has not first obtained his knowledge and instruction from another tier or author. Though we'd all like to believe we are completely creative, we are only so in the minutest degree. All I have learned has come from, or evolved from, someone else. There is really very little new, yet it is always new to us individually as we progress within this art.

It would be foolish to try to list all those who have aided me in my education. There are so many of you. Yet I would be remiss if I did not mention a few who were directly associated with making this work possible.

Before I knew either Harold Campbell of New York City or Ted Niemeyer of New Canaan, Connecticut, I stumbled along on the fly-tying trail. In the beginning, even as now, these two friends gave me my education: one in the ways and means of finding materials, and the other in understanding them and how to put them to best use.

Gus Nevros, my friend, is the photographer who willingly and readily photographed the pertinent descriptions in this volume. Besides Nick Lyons, it was he who prodded me the most to "get to work on that book, you have something different to say." Woly Wolyniec made several valuable drawings included in the book.

Bob Sater nags me every other day about a new pattern or new material he has come across. Half the time I pay little heed, but later I admit that he was right and that I should have paid attention in the first place.

My thanks also to Dave Kashner of the Orvis Company in Manchester, Vermont, and to John Mickievicz of Phoenixville, Pennsylvania, for their contributions pertaining to some of the patterns listed and the methods used.

And though they had nothing directly to do with the writing of this book, it is not out of place to express my gratitude to Mike Migel, Art Flick, Bill Mapel, and Harry Darbee, who in a time past, and of a trying nature, offered their assistance without my having to ask for it and, through their moral support, showed me the way back home.

Unmentioned, but not forgotten, are the countless tiers and fishermen who have shared with me some interesting and enjoyable moments at the vise or pleasant moments waist-high in some free-flowing mountain stream, where we find our retreat from the pressures of a too-fast-flowing world.

This book is dedicated,
with love and gratitude,
to the fraternity of flytiers
and fishermen who,
by their very nature,
have enriched
my own way of life

Introduction

They say there is nothing new under the sun. It isn't so!

It's doubtful that anyone reading Eric Leiser's *Fly-Tying Materials* would guess that his business is supplying materials to flytiers. It is most unusual for a man to give away his hard-earned trade secrets; and when he does, it's definitely *something new*.

Anyone who has tied flies over a period of years will realize how much work and heartache they would have been spared had Eric Leiser's information been available when they first began to tie. Books pertaining to such matters were at best sketchy, and it is doubtful if nearly the amount of help found here would have been found in any *six* of such books. Here you have it *all* in one easily read volume, a book that thoroughly covers the whole field of fly-tying tools and materials.

Fly-tying materials are not cheap, but here is a *supplier*, if you please, who for the price of the book will give you, along with a lot of other good information, many ways to obtain these materials at greatly reduced costs. If his tips are followed, even in part, it won't take you long to save much more money than you paid for this book.

It is amazing that so many flytiers are so much in the dark as to the sources of many of the materials they use in putting together a fly. Here, in two concise chapters, the origin of most fur and feathers is completely covered, much better than I have ever seen it done before, with descriptions of just about every species of feathered or furred creature from which fly-tying materials is derived.

If you have ever opened a container in which you had some exceptionally fine and costly necks or some choice fur stored, only to find that moth larvae or buffalo beetles have been feasting on them, leaving you nothing but a mess, you know what an "all-gone" feeling that can be. Somehow or other, this always seems to happen to your finest and most expensive materials, and with grizzly necks costing from $10 on up and duns (when available!) as high as $50, such an experience hurts. Years ago, when I bought good-quality necks for fifty cents each, excluding duns, it wasn't such a tragedy; but with prices as they are today, to say nothing of the work involved simply to find good-quality materials, it's a disaster. There is no reason in the world for this to happen if you follow Eric Leiser's sound and practical advice.

The descriptions of the various colors of rooster necks will be most helpful, for there is quite a bit of confusion as to the proper color names, excepting of course the more common colors, such as black, brown, and white. This problem is especially true for the duns. I doubt if there is any fly-tying question I've been asked more often than "Just what color is a dun?" Here all this is spelled out in language that anyone can understand.

It would be interesting to know just how many hours of trial and error Eric Leiser spent obtaining the know-how given in his chapter on dyeing and bleaching. Anyone who has spent any time at this job knows what a messy chore it can be if you don't know just what you're doing—to say nothing of the materials that can be ruined. But here you'll learn about each item needed to do a good job, and you'll receive concise instructions on how to get the desired colors. The directions for dyeing necks to a dun shade are extremely helpful; this can be a miserable and frustrating job, and too often necks come out poorly and cannot be used. Not many people would divulge this valuable information, particularly someone in the business of supplying such materials.

The fly-tying tips are excellent—not only for their introduction of some new patterns, but also for the substitutions of some of the materials used in some standard patterns, making them easier to tie and in some cases improving their effectiveness.

The fine photographs are a great help in understanding how to tie the flies, and how to "undress" a rooster or a woodchuck. These latter jobs can be quite messy if you don't have the proper technique.

Many tiers, even some who have been at the game for a number of years, are not aware of all the new synthetic materials available today. Some of them are far superior to those we formerly used, even though it is hard to teach an old dog new tricks. This subject too is amply covered here.

What else can I say?

Only, "Bless you, Eric Leiser! You have done all flytiers—old-timers, recent converts, and those still to take up the art—a *real service.*"

ART FLICK
West Kill, New York

Preface

If ten years ago I had been able to obtain in book form the knowledge I have compiled here, I would have been willing to pay ten times the cost of the present book. It took me all this time to arrive at the ideas and thoughts I offer you, and cost me a hundred times as much as this volume, because I was forced to do the research myself.

Locating sources of material was one of my first problems, and that was naturally followed by what to do with the materials once I had them. For this reason I decided to start with basics and progress through the various difficulties I encountered at each step, such as the preservation and storage, the dyeing and bleaching, and finally the proper use of the hoard I had accumulated. Though these steps are mentioned in few words here, they were projects of some magnitude at the time. Not because they were so difficult, but because there was always the elusive elementary answer, which I had to search for and learn.

This book was written not so much to assist you in the tying of flies, but more to start you thinking on your own. It is intended to help you become creative, and to give you some pointers on approaching the various sources of creativity. One discovery will inevitably lead to another and from there on branch out into a multitude of ideas.

If, for example, you learn from one of the following chapters certain uses of the feathers and quills from the skin of a mallard drake, which you would normally discard as waste, I will feel I have accomplished my purpose.

To many of you some of the processes and procedures mentioned will be familiar, but many will be new or give a new slant on an old method.

The methods, descriptions, and uses listed in the various chapters are the results of my own personal knowledge, as I have acquired it. That there may be more efficient means to attain certain results I have no doubt, and I would be the first to accept them if they were shown to me.

I do not believe in "secrets," since what I know I have only learned from some other source and have then put it to use. What I know, I now wish to share, and I only ask you to do the same and share with other members of our fraternity any knowledge you may have obtained from another source.

Without being maudlin, I like to think that the fraternity of flytiers and fishermen is very special. A bond links us, one to the other, in all things relevant to our pursuits; and this bond should preclude the petty jealousy and envy that produce these "secrets" that others keep to themselves.

The cascading river is our song—
Our reminiscences at dusk our entertainment—
A tired day's sleep our tranquilizer;
And when the naked trees stand guard at the river's edge, the fly-tying
   vise becomes our companion.

Contents

Color insert following page 84

Fly-Tying Materials

1 Raw Material · Feather

If there is a demand for anything, there is usually a supply. If there is no existing supply and the demand is great, the supply will very rapidly be created. There is almost nothing you cannot buy, provided you search for it and are prepared to pay the price.

In the case of materials used for fly tying, *most* of your supplies can be purchased from a reputable mail-order house or a local sporting goods store. More important, however, and that is due to the nature of the material we are discussing, it is very difficult to obtain exactly the quality or shade of the item desired, though your supplier will do the best he can for you.

In all probability, the basic material you need for tying comes from a common source, domestic chickens. These are raised all over the world and are one of the commonest staples on the dinner table of nearly every nationality and creed, with the exception of vegetarians.

Why then does it seem so difficult at times to procure good hackle capes for your tying? The answer is twofold. It is not as difficult for an individual tier to obtain even excellent roosters or hens as it is for some of the mail-order houses dealing in this item. You and I, as individuals, can go out, and little by little, build a beautiful collection of this material just by doing a certain amount of investigation and, in some cases, a bit of work. The second part of the answer comes from our preference, and for most dry-fly tiers that means rooster necks with long, stiff, but especially small hackle feathers. Today nearly everyone wants to tie from size twelve on down to sizes twenty-two, -four and -eight. This is all very well and I for one can't begrudge you your desire for small hackles, since I also would latch on to such a cape were it available in good quality.

Chickens come in various breeds, each of which has not only different coloring but also variations in the feather itself. Some are large, some small, some have large neck hackles with wide fibers that would be excellent for some of our salmon flies, or for tailing, and some have hackles that are a flytier's dream: narrow hackles with a bouncy stiffness.

There are so many breeds of chickens that there is a private association which raises them in competition as you would dogs for a show. Should you know of someone who raises these birds, you might do well to befriend him. For though you could not possibly buy one of his birds while it is still alive, even if you could spend a few hundred dollars for one, should one of his birds collapse of old age or simply die for one reason or another, you can probably get him for nothing, or at most a few dollars. That is, if the owner does not decide to have him stuffed.

Unfortunately, roosters with narrow hackles never seem to come from this country, unless they are specifically raised for show or occasionally for fly tying. This is one of the reasons you will have to resort to materials houses that import them. You may question the feasibility of importing your own from such countries as India, and now also possibly China. You may even be lucky enough to receive a good neck. The only thing that makes this a tough proposition is that there are a number of regulations concerning importation, which is controlled by government agencies. The most important regulation is the requirement by the United States Department of Agriculture: it states that any fowl with feathers on the skin must, upon entering the country, go direct to a decontamination center to be disinfected. Most supply houses have their own decontamination centers, and you could have necks routed to such a one to have the process performed for you at a fixed price per skin.

By this time, between the price of the skin, importation duty, air mail charges, and decontamination fee, the cost of your cape has gone to over a dollar, provided you are purchasing only top-quality merchandise. This sounds much less expensive than the price charged by your supplier, but remember two things and you'll realize why he, your supplier, gets the price he does and which, in most cases, is a fair one.

Your supplier can only expect about 20 to 25 percent of top-grade birds in a shipment. The rest he has to sell at a reduced cost as a number-two or -three grade neck, or wholesale them out at a low price to break even.

As an individual you may be able to obtain a shipment of small quantity the first time you order, but once the exporter realizes you are not a quantity buyer for resale he will not be inclined to send you more of his goods. The exporters in any country depend on the large-quantity importers in the United States for their livelihood. They simply do not wish to jeopardize their position by selling retail in competition with the mail-order house or wholesaler who supplies you.

I have given you the pitfalls of importing, but do not let it stop you from trying if you are inclined to do so. The chapter on importation will cover this subject in more detail.

Now it's time to see what can be done with what is at hand, and for this we are going to take a field trip.

No matter where you live in the United States, or for that matter outside of this country, there is bound to be a poultry farm, or distributor, or simply a small shop carrying live chickens waiting to be butchered and dressed. Ninety-nine percent of these places are within driving distance of your home. To find them, all you have to do is pick up the classified directory and look under poultry or related titles.

Having located the whereabouts of a chicken farm, you should bear in mind only one important consideration, and that is *when* to go. If you happen to be reading this book in the middle of the summer, I strongly urge you not to bother with the chickens at all, because their plumage will leave something to be desired. In fact, with certain exceptions, most of your raw materials in the form of feathers and furs should come from animals during the *prime season,* which in the Northern Hemisphere ranges between late November and early April.

Chickens undergo a molting process whereby they lose their old hackles and start raising new ones. For our purposes we will assume it is January and you've located a likely poultry farm just a few miles from town.

There are two ways you may purchase a chicken—alive or dead. Should you choose the former, you will have to carry along a carton or a burlap sack.

Many flytiers prefer to buy their roosters live, in order that they may do their own skinning of the bird, since the feathers and not the meat are of first importance. However, there are those who have an aversion to holding an animal and then killing it, no matter how humanely this is accomplished. If this is the case with you, by all means have the farmer or butcher do the chore for you. Explain to him, however, that you do not want the feathers cut or damaged, especially those in the neck area. Should you have a further aversion to skinning the bird, he may also accommodate you in this, though there may be an extra charge.

When you arrive at the farm, tell the owner of your intent, and possibly spend a few cordial moments with him asking about his crop or talking about the weather. Rural people have a much more contented way of life and are happier for it. Even if you're in a hurry, don't *you* rush them. They take each day in stride, and many will enjoy your company and a good chat. After these formalities, which are regretfully missing in some of our urban life, you can get down to business.

Chances are one hundred to one you will be looking for a rooster. Therefore, you might ask the farmer if he has any breeding stock to sell. When he takes you to his chicken coops and shows you a few birds, ask also if you can check them out, but let him get the rooster and hold it for you, while you check the plumage. Since you are a flytier you know that you want a bird having stiff neck hackles of a certain size. However, you should also check to see how many pinfeathers are on the bird, how fully grown they are, and if the bird has been fighting excessively with other roosters. All these things will determine the value of the bird to you. For the farmer these factors are of no consequence, since he is, for his part, selling you the meat of the chicken.

If you should come across a breeder of vintage years you may find yourself a fine treasure quite inexpensively. For the farmer the bird will have passed his prime as far as best breeding purposes go, and the meat would not command a good price should he try to sell it elsewhere. You may actually obtain the finest hackle at the least expense. Incidentally, even on an old bird, the meat, though tough, is still edible, and will make either a delicious stew or soup. When you buy direct, you also obtain the fringe benefits.

If, after looking over a number of his birds, you select one, or a few for that matter, but are still on the search for color or type, ask him to refer you to someone who may be raising the particular breed you are after. If you were buying for meat only, he might not give you his competitor's name, but since he has by this time probably decided you are an oddball he may humor you and refer you to his neighbor, or someone who supplies him with his stock. In any event you will have begun an endless trail leading from one chicken farm to another.

Let's assume you've purchased only one rooster. You or the farmer have put the bird into a carton or sack, and now you're taking him home. If you have a live bird, whatever you do, do not, and I stress this strongly, do not take him into the house or apartment. In fact, if you want to eat the by-product, which is a reverse in this case, do not even show the bird to your wife, mother, or any female relations if you can help it. Unless they've been brought up on a farm, they will not, in this day and age, eat any animal they have seen alive.

Depending on where you live, it's best to take the bird either to a shed or garage, where he can be properly taken care of—that is, skinned, dressed, and protected.

RAISING YOUR OWN

Another thought may have occurred to you as you go about collecting materials, and that is the possibility of raising roosters or having someone raise them for you, especially the Plymouth Rock and Andalusian breeds. Though I do not raise any of these birds myself, I have done a bit of research in this area.

Two seasons ago, while traveling through New England, I happened on a very large poultry farm in New Hampshire. The grounds covered quite a few acres and there were many coops and other shelters, besides an extremely large barn for the sole purpose of raising chickens for egg production.

Naturally, being a tier and fisherman, I could not let the opportunity pass without at least some sort of inspection. I was too far away from home to consider any purchase, nor was I prepared for one. But I reasoned that if these people could raise all these chickens, which proved to be in the tens of thousands, they must know something about it.

After having meandered through the outer premises of the farm, I finally asked one of the employees for the owner or supervisor of the concern and was directed to a very cordial and friendly gentleman. We entered into a general conversation, and I told him I was on vacation doing a little fly-fishing, which naturally led to the subject of fly tying, and then of course to feathers. Finally I asked him about the barred Plymouth Rock rooster and its availability. "You can have all the barred Rock cocks you can carry," he said, "free of charge, provided you take them home the day they are born. Otherwise we just eliminate them."

He further explained that since their main business was egg production, they had little use for cocks, with the exception of the breeder stock. This farm happened to be crossing the barred Rock with the Rhode Island Red hen for the sole purpose of producing quantity and quality eggs.

I thought that if I could drive to this farm with a station wagon, take all the cock birds after they were hatched, I could then take them to a friend who owned a piece of land in New York and was familiar with raising chickens, so assuring myself of an endless supply of grizzly necks for my tying needs. I asked the owner how much it would cost to raise a barred Rock for a period of at least two seasons. His answer: "Eight to nine dollars, not counting mortality rate." I was taken aback; this was the price you'd normally pay for just the neck cape alone. I was out to cut expenses, not increase them, which would have been the case, since the friend raising them for me would also be entitled to some remuneration and profit.

The cost of raising chickens happens to be mainly the matter of feed. Most chicks are hatched in the spring and, if raised for food, killed at the end of nine weeks or so. During the summer months the feed bill becomes negligible since chickens can forage for themselves. The real cost comes during the winter, when there are no free pickings, and the birds must therefore be fed, or starve. In addition, they must also be cooped up and protected from the cold. There you have it. These facts pertain mainly to this country and its counterparts; in countries such as India there is no feed bill at all. In those regions chickens help themselves and either make it or do not. Of course, they are an entirely different breed, more closely related to their wild ancestor, the jungle fowl.

Though I have listed some of the problems connected with the raising of chickens, there are tiers, such as Harry Darbee of Livingston Manor, New York, who have done so successfully. The chicken farming business is a study in itself and would require knowledge of breeds, susceptibility to disease, reproduction habits, and feed requirements. It would require an educational background in this particular field to arrive at any degree of success. But it can be done, if you take the time to learn and have the patience and the land to do it with.

If you decide to try raising your own, start on a small scale. No more than half a dozen birds. This will not prove too costly should anything go wrong, and you will still learn as much as if you owned one hundred birds.

Some flytiers who raise their own roosters pluck hackles from certain sections of the neck. These feathers are picked as if they were a crop, approximately three or four times a year, and each time from a different area, so that there is a constant reforestation, as it were, of the plucked or harvested sections. Once a bird has been plucked, however, and bare skin is showing on the rooster, he is kept out of the sunlight; the bird will suffer from sunburn if his natural protection has been taken away from him.

To further make it profitable, the eggs of the hens and the meat of any roosters killed are used as table fare. In addition to the neck cape of the rooster, the saddle and other feathers are also utilized.

If all the above can be accomplished with a low mortality rate, and if birds of special value—such as Blue Andalusians or Plymouth Rocks—are used, the venture will prove profitable.

VARIOUS TYPES AND BREEDS

Though most of the roosters you'll encounter will be large and will have large hackles, occasionally you will run across a choice Bantam breed.

Most of the birds in this country, if raised to maturity and killed in prime season, have excellent hackle—shiny, stiff, and resilient. Their drawback, the long hackle, is really a blessing in disguise when you consider the possibilities of matching shades with one of the smaller imported Indian capes. By using such combinations you will have adequate tailing for number ten and twelve flies from our bird and smaller fibers from the import.

The Rhode Island Red rooster, a domestic bird of a dark mahogany color, has very long hackle feathers ideally suited for the Red Quill pattern.

Do you tie streamer flies? Again, our bird is superior when you are searching for a full saddle hackle feather. And, for the saltwater flytier, the American breed is a boon to his materials collection.

Here is another point to remember, one which very few tiers are aware of: the only parts of a rooster usually sold are the neck and saddle capes, or loose feathers thereof, but there is another part of the bird that has quite useable and slightly different hackles—the wing. Examine the upper portion of the wing where it connects to the body and you will find shorter, yet extremely stiff-fibered, feathers, which have various uses, including tailing. And though no one seems to consider the wing pointers for tying, they are useable for the winging of certain patterns, and have the obvious quill materials for bodies as well.

What about the tail? Depending on the breed of bird you obtain, the tail feathers, which are fairly long, have in their quill, after stripping, various shadings and segmentations. Some are fairly thick near the butt, yet once soaked, any portion can be used for ribbing and quill bodies, all depending on your pattern and what you intend to use it for.

The uses found in one bird are endless, and I will add here that this is the case with most of the materials we use today, whether they come from feather or fur. Most of them are overlooked, and we will cover them in some detail in ensuing chapters. The point I am trying to make here is that when you do skin out a bird, rooster or hen, do the *entire* bird. All the feathers, plus the quill sections, right down to the fluffy down are valuable.

Though you will find various sizes and shadings in the roosters you come across, the ones you will most likely encounter are the barred Plymouth Rock, with its gray and white marking; the White Leghorn, which you can dye into a blue dun, or any shade for that matter; the New Hampshire Red, of a chestnut brown shade; the Rhode Island Red, a much darker brown; perhaps some Orpingtons, Andalusians, Wyandottes, or Brahmas. It all depends on the farmer and his selection of breed. However, as I stated earlier, you will be able to track down some of the rarer breeds, or more desirable strains, if you make a crusade of it. Check the advertisements in the outdoor magazines or related printed matter, to see where game farms and breeding establishments are located, and they in turn may advise you who carries certain breeds you are interested in.

One last type very worthy of mention is the rooster of the fighting-cock class. This particular strain of chicken is raised and sold more for show than for fighting, especially since cockfights are generally outlawed in the United States. However, these fights still do exist, and, like gambling, there is much of it going on despite the prohibitions set forth by the various legislatures. I am against cruelty to animals in any form; if an animal is to be killed, whether for food or some other legitimate reason, it should then be done as swiftly and humanely as possible. I do not attend cockfights, nor do I know where they are held. Still, if you know of someone connected with these affairs, even if he is only a spectator, you might ask him to bring you some of the "losers." These will be the dead birds that have been defeated and left for the garbage. A fighting cock, alive, is an extremely expensive bird, especially if he is a good one. Yet, even the best meet their downfall in these arenas and, for the owner, become worthless.

Should you be fortunate enough to obtain some of these strains of roosters, you will be pleased to find that they have a very high quality hackle, and the tailing material on them is highly prized. In addition, you will have played a small part in the game of conservation, since the loser will not have succumbed completely in vain. Much use will be found for the feathers on his skin.

Besides being very rewarding as far as building your materials collection, this search for the rooster, and the unusual aspects of exceptional good fortune now and again, becomes an exciting enterprise for its own sake.

OTHER FEATHER SOURCES

Once you have gotten the knack of chasing after chickens, you will very likely and quite naturally start looking into other sources of raw material in this area of feathers. After the basic neck cape of the chicken, probably the most sought-after feathers come from the duck, both domestic and wild.

The domestic duck, which is white, can be procured in the same manner as the rooster. Go to a duck farm and repeat the procedure you used in obtaining the chicken. Here again, the entire skin can be utilized. Not only the wings for the Royal Coachman and other patterns, but also the breast and side feathers have their uses.

Other than the common white duck, I have come across very few domestically raised fowl in this area, with the possible exceptions of the Muscovy and, of course, the mallard.

The case of the mallard is somewhat peculiar since it can be raised domestically with a special license, or obtained in the wild during legal gunning season. In either case there may be restrictions or stipulations regarding its sale, and these legalities should be checked locally.

Except for the wood duck, the mallard is the most sought-after duck. It is common enough, so you should have few problems securing one. However, your chances with the mallard, wood duck, and other birds of this family are greater if you also happen to be a duck hunter, or the friend of one, since that is where most of these birds are obtained. If neither of these situations applies to you there is one other recourse, and that is to go to a game preserve.

Game preserves are places designed to allow the hunter to bag his ducks, and other game, at a fixed fee, ranging anywhere from four to five dollars a bird and up. It all depends on the individual preserve. These establishments buy and raise their own stock, and are therefore not governed, except by license and banding regulations, by the state and federal laws. Hunting seasons, at least in the state of New York, do not apply to a game preserve.

I have absolutely no idea how many birds are released by these farms each year for the hunters' pleasure, but they are quite numerous. In many cases, wounded birds are found after a client has left, in which case they are humanely killed. These excess birds accumulate in a preserve. Investigate these farms and you may come home with more than you need in the way of feathers and bird skins. The duck that game preserves usually stock is the mallard, though such birds as pheasants and quail may also be released from the same farm.

The most sought-after ducks are, of course, the American wood duck and its Far Eastern cousin the mandarin. I might add here that when I speak of ducks or other birds, I am generally referring to the drake or male of the species; nature has endowed the male with all the beautiful colors and left the female a bit on the drab side. There is a purpose in this since it is the fair, in this case a misnomer, sex of the bird kingdom that needs a certain amount of camouflage to protect the young she is raising in the wild. Hen ducks have some value, but in most cases they are not as desirable as the male.

There is so little difference between the mandarin and the American wood duck that neither is prized above the other. They are equally sought for their lemon brown side feathers, which are used in more patterns than I'd care to list.

The wood duck, either breed, cannot be purchased as you would a chicken. You will be able to obtain them from a fly-tying materials house should these establishments have them in stock, or they can be collected by yourself or a friend during legal hunting season. In some areas, especially the southeastern and southwestern regions nearer the coasts, these birds are fairly common. Up north, though they do fly through their ancestral migratory routes, they sometimes leave before the hunting season opens, depending on weather conditions. An early cold spell will move them out much sooner than other species of ducks.

In the matter of begging duck skins from a hunting buddy, the extent of your fortune will, in large, depend on whether he is also a fishing partner or not. If he is, you will be able to receive the entire skin of the duck; otherwise you may wind up with a bag full of loose feathers, since he may prefer to pluck his duck and roast him with the skin intact, as opposed to filleting him. In the case of the wood duck the plucking procedure will be no great calamity because you are mainly interested in those prized lemon feathers. These are easy enough to pluck from the skin in a clump, and kept apart from the rest of the bird's plumage, so you won't have too much sorting to do. Whether mixed in with other feathers or not, this particular plumage is worth the time it takes to sort them out.

Besides the mallard and the wood duck, there are many other kinds of ducks hunted in the United States, and each and every one of them will be of value to you as a flytier.

Procure from your friends any and all of these duck skins, wing quills, or feathers. Some of the species of ducks hunted include the following: widgeon, pintail, black duck (mallard), gadwall, teal, redhead, canvasback, scaup, coot, bufflehead, and mergansers.

Though there are more on the list, and subspecies of the above named, it is best to check the federal regulations as to which can be hunted and the limits in your particular area. Since ducks are a migratory bird, they are controlled by a federal agency under the Fish and Wildlife Division. Hunting may be allowed for a certain species where the particular breed is not endangered, and the species totally protected in other areas because of its scarcity.

Though they do not seem to be used as extensively as ducks for fly tying, the larger relative of this bird, the goose, and their species are very valuable in certain tying operations, and in quite a few patterns of flies. What goes for the duck, goes for the goose: a legally shot wild goose that is thrown in the garbage is just pure waste. Use the feathers.

Geese of the domestic variety are mostly white, and to obtain them you simply go on a goose chase, as you did with the chicken. Domestic goose is the most likely substitute for swan, now a prohibited bird.

Rounding out the fowl family are the guinea fowl, which is domestically raised, though inherently wild, and the various species of pheasants.

Two of the most important pheasants used in fly tying are the golden and the silver pheasant.

The golden pheasant is prized primarily for its cape, from which the barred black and orange-red tippets are procured and used for tailing, and the crest, or topknot, which is golden and slightly curved, making it excellent material for topping on streamer flies.

The silver pheasant is white with black barring; mainly the body feathers are used as cheeking in streamer flies.

Hunting of the above birds is illegal. Many, however, are raised in this country for show. For these two pheasants you will have to rely on your supply house.

Golden pheasant   Silver pheasant

The only pheasant regularly hunted in nearly every state, and also raised for commercial purposes, is the Chinese or English ringneck. Your course is the same as before: either buy them from a farm or preserve, or beg one from your hunting friends.

Peafowl are pheasants of an Asian or East Indian variety. Most zoos or farms exhibiting them usually show only the peacock, the brilliantly colored male, with its fanlike tail.

This bird may be obtained in the United States, but your sources here are scattered and perhaps more costly if you are looking for the eyed tail only. Purchase these direct from a materials house since they are plentiful and relatively inexpensive.

Peafowl are imported from India. Actually, the only parts brought in are the tails and swords of the cock; the whole skin is never imported simply because Indian law prohibits its exportation. You may believe that the "eyed" tails are plucked from this bird, and in some cases they are. Most of the tails you buy, however, are collected by the natives after the bird has shed these feathers during molting season. They are then bundled up like sheaves of wheat and sold to a quantity buyer for a few cents, who in turn sells them on an export quota to all parts of the world.

In India the peafowl is a sacred bird and is not used for food, although the meat is very good. Whether the less advantaged sections of that country adhere to this law I do not know, but I would surmise that an empty stomach may dent Indian policy a little here and there along with the overproduced peafowl.

RIngneck pheasant

Lady Amherst pheasant

The only reason you should be on the lookout for a whole skin is that these birds do have wings, and these extremities have a certain few cinnamon-colored wing quills you will not find on any other bird. For this your best source will be a farm or store dealing in show birds. Naturally, some die, and you may find this bird at no cost whatever.

If I tried to tie without turkey feathers I would be leaving a large gap in the tying of some of my favorite patterns. This domesticated bird is a direct descendant of the wild turkey, once very abundant in this land. The species most used is the bird with brown coloration, with its speckled center-wing quills and black and white barred pointers.

This and the wild turkey, which is making a strong comeback in many states and is once again legally hunted, depending on the area, are much alike, except that the wild turkey has a desirable extra sheen in some of its smaller tail and back feathers. Both are highly prized, not only because of the feather color and its use in various patterns, but also because the fibers of the feathers marry very well in the winging of certain imitations.

Crossbreeding has produced some off shades of this species and, while much in demand, they are not common. Cinnamon and gray turkey tails are two of the more difficult feathers to come by, but if you can obtain some don't pass them up. They are fine shades for quill bodies and wing cases.

The white turkey is being bred more and more for market, and here you have a fine source of supply, both as is and for dyeing to needed shades.

One of the best times to go about procuring turkey feathers is obviously just before Thanksgiving; at that time of the year they are slaughtered by the millions, and they have just started to take on their winter plumage.

You will indeed be fortunate if you are able to secure a wild turkey, since very few hunters score on this elusive bird, even in areas of plenty.

Some tiers may not be aware of the fact that today marabou comes from the turkey and not the marabou stork, as was the case many years ago. Marabou is the soft, fluffy, turkey body feather that has not formed the squared-off feather tip. These feathers, of course, would come from the white turkey. They dye fairly easily into any desired color.

This covers most of the domestic field and the plumage of raised stock. But though we have covered some of their wild cousins, there are other bird skins and feathers you should be on the lookout for. Some will come under game laws, and some are considered pests. The only thing you have to remember is that if it flies, and can be legally and conservatively obtained, it will be useable.

Since laws on game birds and pest species vary from one state to another, I remind you again to check your local and state laws covering the particular bird. A pest in one state may be protected in another, and vice versa. Laws may also be revised from year to year, so be sure to check current regulations.

In general, all songbirds are completely protected, and even their possession may be illegal in some states. Though you yourself may not have killed the bird, picking him up off the highway, where he met his demise while diving at an automobile, may be an illegal act. (In this regard I think there is a waste, since the bird in question will just be lost through decay, when some use may be had from its plumage.)

Following is a listing of birds available to you through your friend, the hunter:

GROUSE. A game bird quite common in most northern states and actually a wild chicken, since he also belongs to the fowl family. Feathers are used mostly for nymphs. Both brown and gray body feathers will be found on this bird, though there may be a predominance of one shade over the other, depending on the individual bird, or the particular breed, the two most common being the ruffed and the blue grouse.

This bird is somewhat, but not exactly, like its European counterpart the partridge, although in the New England states many hunters refer to our native grouse as "partridge."

Unfortunately, the English partridge, like other wild birds, is not importable.

QUAIL. There are a number of species of this game bird, the most common of which is the bobwhite quail. Though not often mentioned in fly-tying books, this bird, and more especially some of its far western relatives such as the California quail, scaled quail, and Gambel's quail, takes on a little more importance these days because of the feathers in the neck area, which can be used as a substitute for the prohibited jungle cock.

The bobwhite, found abundantly in the eastern and southern states, is readily obtainable through hunting companions. All of the western varieties, which are much more colorful, are not so easily obtained due to their limited area and numbers. If, however, you can arrange a trade for some of these, it will be a valuable addition to your materials collection.

WOODCOCK. This bird is also covered by the federal migratory regulations, while simultaneously controlled by state limits and seasons. It is different from the English woodcock, in that it lacks the barring on the wing section often desirable for certain patterns. Nevertheless, it is quite a useful bird for the flytier.

CROW. I doubt if this bird is protected in any of our states, simply because it is so plentiful and such a pest that some communities unite at times to bring its population down to a bearable level.

It is one of the most intelligent and wary of our feathered wildlife, and though hunted as a varmint, it will rarely come within range of a gun. Most farmers, should you hunt, will give you permission to go afield on their land if you tell them you'd like to do a little crow shooting. The crow is a fairly large bird with glossy, black plumage over its entire body. There are many uses for this bird.

STARLING. Sometimes referred to as English starling, since that is where they originated. These birds, approximately three hundred and fifty of them, were brought into this country on an experimental basis, for what reason I don't know. They were released in New York and have since spread as far west as the Rockies. Flytiers may cheer, but this was one of our more unfortunate imports. Starlings are extremely aggressive and detrimental to a number of our native songbirds. They are therefore considered pests in most states.

Because they are fairly small, it is probably best to take them with .22 caliber bird shot. If you do not hunt, ask your friends to do some target shooting on them, so that they can sharpen their aim for the upcoming duck season.

ENGLISH SPARROW. Like the starling, a pest—though smaller.

At this point you may begin to wonder why you need all these birds. Because fly tying is a creative and constantly changing art. Birds, even within their own species, are so different from one another that the more collectibles you have, the more variations you will be able to perform on your patterns.

There is also the matter of substitutes. We are mainly dealing in this book with domestic and wildlife birds and animals you are likely to obtain, the uses of which will be discussed later. However, just for an example, did you know that the wing quills of the starling would make a stronger body than the peacock quill when the outer layer is soaked and stripped down? Or for very fine winging on small flies the sparrow gives you a more lifelike imitation on certain patterns? Try a few experiments and see for yourself.

PIGEON. In New York State pigeons in the wild state may be shot, since they are considered pests. Unfortunately, most of the pigeons in the wild state seem to make their homes in the large cities, where the discharge of firearms is prohibited. This is just as well, since the birds that dwell in urban areas are generally diseased. I would suggest, therefore, that you locate some in rural sections.

The pigeon is most desirable because different birds provide many different shades of coloration. No two ever seem to be the same color.

MAGPIE. What the crow is in the East, the magpie is in the West—namely, a pest, but with much more color. Since birds with some of the brighter colors are getting more difficult to obtain, it would be wise to add a few magpies to your collection if you can.

I have listed but a few of the domestic and wildlife birds available to you. Some of the other species, their uses, and substitutions will be listed in a later chapter.

Always remember: Check your local regulations concerning the collecting of various game and pest birds. If the birds are available to you, whether I have mentioned them or not, add them to your stockpile. All of them have a use.

2 Raw Material · Fur

In the domestic field, one of the easiest items to obtain, and one of the most used, is the calf tail, which is sometimes referred to as kip or impala.

A calf is a baby cow or bull, and it is killed early because its meat, veal, is very tender. Many calves are slaughtered for this purpose, and there is a twofold reason: the farmer raising the beef avoids an excessive feed bill, and he also receives a much higher price for the meat.

Each week, calves are killed in slaughterhouses by the thousands. Every part, even the skin, of the animal is utilized—except for the tail. This is usually discarded or thrown in a heap to be sold as waste to the glue factory.

How many tails do you need? Visit a slaughterhouse, and for the few that you require they will probably not even charge you. You will be getting the tail with the bone still in it, which means you will have to skin it out. If you do this while the tail is still fresh, the skin will come off very easily. If you decide to wait for the weekend, or when you have some spare time, I advise you to wrap your tails in a poly bag and place them in your freezer until you can get at them. This will keep them fresh for skinning—after they have been thawed out again, of course.

There are slaughterhouses near, or on the outskirts of, most large cities. A telephone call or a sincere letter will get you what you want. If they should charge you, or want you to take a certain quantity at so much per tail, which is usually around five or six cents, all you have to do is get a few of your fly-tying friends together, order the tails, and divide the "spoils."

Incidentally, calf tails come not only in natural white, which will be used as such and dyed, but also in natural black and tan, with a few beige shades thrown in. Some will have longer hair, excellent for streamers, while others will be of standard size for winging material.

Other animals in the domestic field include the horse, the pig, and the sheep.

The only worthwhile tying material on the horse comes from his tail, the strands of which provide excellent ribbing material.

You would not think there would be much use from a pig, nor think of this animal as having fur, which it does have on its belly. This is the part you want if you can obtain it. The fur on the underside of the pig is soft and pinkish, very desirable as a tying material.

There is no need to bother with sheep, since you can buy all the pure wool you want, in all colors, in your local department store.

Now the only domestics we have left are those of the pet variety, and heaven help you if anyone even suspects you have an ulterior motive or design in this area. About the only thing you can do, if the species has desirable fur qualities, is to clip a small swatch while either Rover or Cleopatra is asleep. Whatever you do, do not cut so large a piece that it is noticeable. While you will not hurt the animal in any way, physically or psychologically, there may be drastic consequences if someone thinks you've scarred your pet. Provided you take from different areas on the animal, and always let the hair or fur grow back at the previous section of snipping, think what an endless supply you can harvest if you are careful.

As you can see, with few exceptions there is little available from domestic animals in comparison to what the feathered group provides. Therefore, for some of our supply, we will simply have to go afield.

I live in New York State, and besides fly tying and fishing, I enjoy the sport of hunting. If you travel by car just forty minutes away from the city's limits, you can fish in pure clear streams that contain trout, and be so surrounded by trees and wildlife that you would mistake the country for a remote wilderness area, untouched by man. Did you know that New York State has more square miles of land put aside as "forever wild" than any other state in the union? Most of this land is concentrated in the Adirondack and Catskill parks, the mountains of which are the birthplace for such trout streams as the Beaverkill, the Willowemoc, the Esopus, the Ausable, the Saranac, and a thousand lesser known rivers.

I enjoy hunting, but only under a self-imposed set of rules. I will not shoot anything I don't intend to eat, or use. To be afield alone, and pursue my quarry with whatever woods knowledge the years have left me, is almost an end in itself. More escapes me than I collect.

If you are not a hunter, and do not intend to become one, you are not entirely restricted to begging for the skins of certain animals, in order to stock your materials supply; there are other ways to help fill your fly-tying needs.

Probably the most hunted of all big game animals in the United States, and also one of the most used in fly tying, is the white-tailed deer. Most states have a harvestable population of these, some in larger numbers than others. For some reason, I have found the tail and body hair of the eastern and northeastern whitetail of better texture than those of the western, midwestern, and southern states. Pennsylvania and New York deer are especially desirable.

For the nonhunter, the easiest way to procure a skin or a number of tails, other than from hunting friends, is to find out when the deer season takes place in your state, and then go to some of the butcher houses in your vicinity. Many hunters neither know how nor want to do their own cutting of venison for the table, and therefore leave it to the experts. Few hunters even bother with the skin of the animal, fewer save it. The establishments that do the butchering may save the skins for tanneries, since they can realize a small side profit from its sale. In this case it may cost you three dollars for an entire skin. The tails can usually be had for nothing, since they are not used by the tanneries for gloves, jackets, or other buckskin-type apparel. One skin will give you enough body hair for a lifetime of tying, but you undoubtedly will require more than one tail, if only because you will need some dyed shades in addition to the natural white and brown.

In this country we have three kinds of deer, namely the whitetail, the mule deer, and the California blacktail. While all are suitable, the whitetail is preferable. Also belonging to the deer family as a group are the elk, moose, and caribou. Our western antelope is of a different species altogether. All of the above are desirable for varying reasons.

The largest of these animals is the moose, and while it is not as populous as it once was, many hunters still seek it in Canada, so that you will come across it now and again. Generally, hunters do not bring back a whole moose because of its size. Ask your friends to save you the mane, which is one of the more important materials you'll use in fly tying.

Also hunted in Canada is the caribou, and here you'll want some of the body hair, which is of a finer texture than other deer hair. For very small clipped-body flies, such as the Irresistible and the Rat-faced McDougall, this material is excellent.

Elk, though still hunted in some of our western states, is not too easy to obtain directly. Again, few hunters bring back an entire hide. Though extremely useful, and a material that can be dyed different shades, elk is difficult to acquire. Unless you live in one of the western states where it is hunted, it will be a rare event if you find an elk hunter who will oblige you.

The same applies to the antelope, also a western resident. Body hair on this animal is heavier and coarser than that of deer, but is used in the tying of the Spuddler, a very effective pattern. Its use, of course, does not end there.

Also hunted as big game are members of the bear family, the black bear being the most common and, fortunately, the most desirable. However, because of the elusive qualities of bears in general, the success ratio is small among hunters. The hunter who scores on this animal prizes his trophy and in many instances has a rug made out of the skin. In this case, all you are likely to obtain are the trimmings. But that is better than no bear at all.

Alaska is about the only place left to hunt the grizzly and the brown bear. So few are taken each year that your chances in this area are slim, but, should the occasion arise, do not pass up any of this fine fur and hair.

Even scarcer, and very highly prized, are mountain sheep and goats. I am still looking for a scrap of their hide, thus far without any luck.

Most of your accumulations of fur and hair will come from animals classified as small game. Though they may vary in different states, the hunted species are generally basic—rabbit, squirrel, fox, woodchuck, and the like. Some will be game animals with a season and limit, and others will come under the category of varmints. Again, you will either hunt them yourself, or ask someone to bring you the skin of the animal.

ROAD HUNTING

You do not have to be a hunter to be a "road hunter." There are a few restrictions, especially on game animals, that will prevent you from collecting them, but by and large, if you keep a sharp eye out, you will find enough to add to your growing collection.

Besides myself, I have a few friends who, as they drive along the countryside to their favorite streams, or are just out for a Sunday drive, have an uncannily trained right eye that can spot an animal as they are moving along. Identification becomes relatively easy after a little experience. Of course if you are on a super-highway you will not be able to stop, but on most of the secondary roads there is usually a shoulder, and enough room to park the car and go back and inspect the animal or bird that has been the victim of a hit-and-run driver. In this case there is no law covering the fate of the animal in question since they usually dart in front of an automobile without warning. (Whatever you do, should a small animal recklessly run across your path while you're at the wheel, do not try to swerve. You can possibly cause an accident. If there is enough room and no other traffic is near you, by all means try to avoid hitting it.)

Most of the animals you see along the roadside have met their ends sometime during the past evening or early morning, when they are most active. How long a particular animal has been dead can in part be determined, should it be during the warmer months, by the number of flies that have gathered on the carcass, or from the odor (indicating a certain ripeness). You will have to decide whether it is worth your while to spend the time to clean and skin it.

In my station wagon I always carry a pair of pruning shears, a large plastic bag, and a knife for just these occasions when I find some desirable piece of feather or fur still attached to a body, along the roadside. If I am going fishing I also usually carry some frozen iced cans in the food cabinet, which serves the dual purpose of refrigerating the lunch and preserving any possible "find." This all may sound a little weird to you at first, but believe me, it is all mind over matter. If you use your judgment, which will develop with training and percep-tion, you will be able to tell which bird or animal to keep, and which to forget. I have seen some of the most beautiful skins collected this way by a friend of mine. Incidentally, if *you* should happen to kill wildlife, do not hesitate at all to go back and skin it out.

Road hunting is done mostly with wild game in the varmint or pest class, since even possession of an out-of-season bird or mammal may make you liable for a fine. Again, your local regulations will clear this up. There may be a chance you can keep even a game animal if you report it to a conservation officer, though in the case of larger species, such as deer, I don't think you will get permission. It does no harm to ask, in any event.

I can recall one occasion where I was twice fortunate. It happened while driv-ing along Route 30 at a point where this road encircles the Pepacton reservoir, which is one of the watershed impoundments for the metropolitan area. I had been able to collect a woodchuck tail, which I use for the Au Sable Wulff pat-tern, of prime condition and excellent marking. Not many hours later, while waiting for my wife to settle us in the motel, I went out in the back woodlot, and while scouting around, came across a porcupine, also a varmint in New York State. If it were not for their fine meat and useable quills and bristles, I doubt if I would ever bother to shoot one, since they are slow and have no defense against man. The quills are the only way they can protect themselves against predators, and a porcupine accomplishes this simply by wrapping himself up in a ball, and letting any would-be attacker take a bite. Most predators are quickly discouraged.

I shot the porcupine with a small-caliber firearm and gutted him on the spot, then brought my prize back to my wife. She is so used to my doing these seemingly weird things that it no longer seems to bother her; in fact, since darkness had approached, she held the flashlight while I skinned the animal out. The way to skin a porcupine is "very carefully."

Though I have seen numerous and various kinds of birds along the roadside, I have on only one occasion been able to find a crow, and that was a young one. These birds seem to have a built-in radar system that enables them to clear out before any passing vehicle can possibly clip them. Then, as soon as the car has gone past, they go right back to feeding on whatever they have found on the highway.

For those of you who hunt, whether in the game class or for varmints, remember these few tips:

1. Clean and skin your game as soon as possible.
2. Try to keep it cool until you arrive home.
3. Protect it from flies and other vermin.

This last holds especially true for woodchuck hunters, who are usually out during the warm weather.

When hunting 'chucks, I literally run toward a downed animal and process it on the spot. Because of the high-velocity, flat-shooting, but light-grained cartridge used the bullet explodes upon impact. There is a sound safety factor involved in the use of this type of cartridge: because of the slug blowup, ricochet is eliminated, whether the bullet hits the animal or the background. However, since it does explode, it results in a fairly large hole in the 'chuck, thus attracting blowflies from quite a distance.

Since I enjoy eating groundhog meat, I keep my animal as clean as possible; the meat is tender, delicious, and all the other adjectives you would use in describing a prime piece of beef. After all, these animals feed on only the best hay the farmer makes available to his cows.

Once I have cleaned a 'chuck I've shot, I slip him into a large plastic bag, to keep the flies from depositing their eggs. If you have ever seen maggots develop on a raw piece of fur, remember they came from those flies you let get to your animal. After cleaning and bagging, I put my game into the food chest in the wagon, where I always keep some iced cans.

After gutting a rabbit or squirrel, let the animal hang a short while, depending on weather conditions. This will permit some of the lice, fleas, or other parasites to depart, since they lose interest in a body that has lost its warmth. Hunting for small game usually occurs during the colder months, and blowflies and such will have disappeared.

TAXIDERMISTS AND FURRIERS

It's time to explore two other sources, where you do not have to be afield to obtain your supplies—the taxidermist and the furrier. Unless you live near one of the larger cities, chances are that there will not be a furrier doing business near you, though you may find a trapper who supplies him. If this is the case, the trapper will gladly sell you some skins either at, or slightly more than, the price he is obtaining from the furrier. These will be some of the finest skins you can obtain, since they are prime and usually untanned. You do not even have to do your own skinning.

If you live near one of our larger cities, it would pay to check the classified telephone book for that area and look under Fur or Furriers. Take a spare day and make the trip: you may wind up with a goldmine of cuttings, damaged furs, and possibly some pieces of exotic animals you have never even heard of. A furrier depends entirely on quality fur for the making of various coats and apparel. If a piece of fur mismatches, or has a mark or scarring in the wrong place, it cannot be used, and is either discarded or sold as piece goods by the pound to a dealer trading in such cuttings.

Prices by the pound for cuttings will vary from two to four dollars. Can you imagine how much dubbing is to be had in one pound of mixed fur? A furrier may also have some untanned hides lying around which he will sell you very cheaply because the trap that caught the animal has ruined a certain section of prime fur. Since furriers deal in quantity they will buy "lots" of these furs, and upon checking, put the damaged skins aside. It does not pay to have them tanned. There are also cases where a fur will come back from the tannery in a damaged condition. In this case your man will be glad to have back his cost. There are, as you can see, many reasons why a furrier has some waste, and many reasons why you should check out this source. Some common furs you might obtain are muskrat, mink, raccoon, fox, opossum, fitch, and even such rarer furs as seal, sable, and kangaroo.

Wherever there is fishing or hunting there is a taxidermist. Who of us, provided he can afford it, does not want a prize trophy mounted on his wall, in order to do a little, well-earned bragging to our friends and guests, besides reminiscing on all the details and events that occurred in the taking of the particular fish or game.

That is why taxidermists are in business, and there are quite a few of them. I doubt if you have to go very far to find one no matter where you live. Like the furrier, a taxidermist also has some waste attached to his work. If he is mounting the head of a deer or an elk, or making a rug from a black bear, he has to do some trimming to get the animal into presentable shape for his client's wall or floor.

A taxidermist will not only do work on local game, but in many cases be shaping a skin for a client that has been hunting in Canada, Asia, or Africa. Here again, you may find some of the rarer hairs and furs. It would not hurt to tell him you are a fisherman, and that when you finally take that "lunker" brown, you would like him to have it mounted for you. Many taxidermists are fishermen themselves, and enlightening him as to your purpose may produce a number of desirables for your collection. Should you come home with a box full of tier's gold, it won't hurt to send him some of your flies. Even if he does not fish, they may make a nice decoration on *his* wall.

If you pursue the methods of obtaining feathers and furs outlined in the preceding pages, you should soon have a formidable collection. You will, in fact, wind up with more than you need. What do you do in that case?

Where you live will in some measure determine the kind of materials you have accumulated; you may have an overabundance of certain furs and feathers that another tier has difficulty obtaining. There are ways you can trade or sell your excess, and exchange it for the items you lack, either by a strict trade or on a cash basis.

Some of your seemingly more common items, such as squirrel tails, deer tails, or hair, may in most instances even be traded to a fly-tying materials house. Though this may seem strange, there are some items that supply houses can never get enough quantity of to supply other tiers. Many will either give you cash or a trade allowance. The easiest way to ascertain their needs is to send for a copy of their catalog and see what furs and feathers they carry. A letter offering your surplus will, in most cases, be very welcome.

You need not worry about putting your favorite materials house out of business by doing your own collecting. Most of them would rather sell you the manufactured items anyway. Hackle necks, expensive as they may be, yield less profit than you may imagine. Nor do the companies enjoy having to pack all those loose feathers and furs, besides storing large quantities, which invariably lead to infestations of one sort or another. They do their best to protect their goods, but raw materials for a large concern are considered a perishable item; it is much easier to sell the tools, hooks, rods, reels, and lines. They carry these because they are basic and needed by the tier.

3 Tying Materials · General

A casual glance at the catalogs of a few supply houses will substantiate the fact that the following list of materials is fairly basic to tiers everywhere.

THREAD

Today there is still a difference of opinion over which is the better thread: silk or nylon? The arguments began when nylon thread was first manufactured.

Nylon stretches, silk does not; but the amount that it does is so negligible in fly tying as to be hardly worth debating. Both are equally fine, and if you are out to cut a few corners, nylon is cheaper.

Both nylon and silk thread may be had in sizes from A to 6/o, silk to 9/o. If you have ever wondered about these size designations, the following explanation should clear it up.

After size A, which is the largest used in fly tying, thread diameters get smaller as the number of zeros are added. Thus, size oo, which is the next smallest after size A, is followed in turn by size ooo, oooo, ooooo, oooooo, ooooooo, ooooooo, and ooooooooo. Since it gets tedious to add all these zeros, manufacturers have simply added a number followed by a slash to indicate whether a thread should be a "three ought" or "six ought." Thread sizes from the largest to the smallest now read: A, 2/o, 3/o, 4/o, 5/o, 6/o, 7/o, 8/o, and 9/o.

For the tying of dry flies the finest in threads are used, mostly from 6/o to 9/o. Wets and nymphs will generally be tied with 4/o, though occasionally either a 3/o or 5/o. Streamers, bucktails, and saltwater flies take the larger sizes, such as A and 2/o.

Only black and white threads are made all the way down to a size 6/o or 9/o, with few exceptions. The reason for this is that the thread manufacturers do not make their living off flytiers. The bulk of their sales are in millinery and garment

Thread

making. Only one company I know of specializes in a thread of various colors used by flytiers. It produces Herb Howard prewaxed nylon thread—which is made of a special twist nylon in order to lie flat—in the following colors: black, white, gray, brown, olive, red, yellow, cream, and fire-orange. The size of this thread is a 7/o. The Herb Howard thread is probably the most commonly used by fly-tiers today, for all kinds of tying.

When buying thread, always try to purchase that which is wound on a standard-sized spool. It will then fit most of the bobbins, manufactured to hold them.

On a standard spool, a fine thread can be had in quantities of fifty to five hundred yards. If you do a fair amount of tying it is economical to buy the latter. The labor price varies very little whether you buy one or the other, since they both must be wound.

Other threads on the market are Nymph thread and Monocord, also used on nymphs. These threads are manufactured to lie flat and not bulk up the fly. Nymph thread by Gudebrod comes in various shades in size 6/o. Belding Corti-celli's Monocord, also in colors, may be had in sizes A and 3/o.

CHENILLE, FLOSSES, AND WOOLS

CHENILLE. One of the most commonly used materials in fly tying, especially for wet flies and streamers, this yarn comes in so many sizes and colors that most fly-tying houses cannot carry all of them.

Chenille can be made so fine as to appear like a fuzzy piece of thread or so large in diameter that it can be made into leis, the kind Hawaiians throw around your neck. For the flytier it is generally sold in five or six sizes, namely oo, o, 1, 2, 3, and possibly 4. Size oo is the smallest.

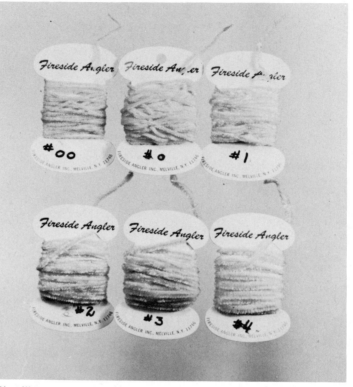

Chenille

Chenille is usually a rayon or silk fiber wound onto a thread core. It is also possible for the manufacturer to wind tinsel, or intermingle tinsel and rayon, to produce what is called sparkle, or tinsel chenille. One of the most common used in patterns is a black chenille having an oval tinsel wound through the chenille in a natural spiral.

Pure tinsel chenille does not have either rayon or silk entwined with it. It makes a very glittery effect, both for fishermen and Christmas trees.

For the saltwater and steelhead fisherman, chenille now comes in all the fluorescent shades, such as red, yellow, orange, white, blue, green, and hot pink. It makes an exceptional attractor.

FLOSS. Again, the main use is in streamers, wets, and nymphs. Manufactured in either silk or nylon, it can be purchased in single- and four-stranded spools.

The four-strand spool can be wound in bulk for a streamer, or singly for the smaller wets and nymph patterns.

Besides the standard types of floss there is on the market today a yarn called Acetate Floss, which is used in conjunction with an acetone solution. The combination has been expressly offered to the flytier for the making of flat-bodied nymphs. It works this way: having wound the acetate floss onto the hook shank, it is then tied down, and the acetone applied to the floss body. When the chemical reaction starts between the floss and the solution, the body of the nymph can be shaped with a pair of pliers to any form desired.

I have found acetate floss excellent just as it is in the forming of tapered streamer bodies, because of its bulky size and its spreadability. It works best in a bobbin.

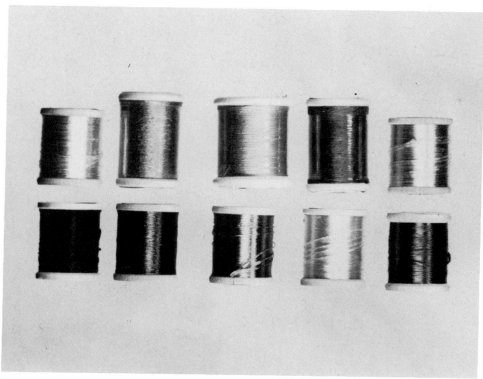

Floss

WOOL. Sold by every fly-tying materials house and also every department store. If one concern does not have the particular shade you are looking for, another will. Probably because there are more women knitting than fishermen tying flies, it is made in just about every color imaginable.

Whether it is single, double, or four stranded, what you want is that made of 100 percent virgin wool.

SPUN FUR. This is actually true angora rabbit fur spun into a yarn. If you are using rabbit as a dubbing, spun fur comes already prepared for you. It can be tied in, or twisted onto the thread in the normal dubbing fashion. It comes in a variety of shades.

PLUMAGE

Feathers from both domestic and wild birds are sold prepackaged by all mail-order houses dealing in fly-tying materials. Certain of these materials will be treated in complete detail in other chapters, but a brief listing here is in order.

PEACOCK. From this bird the three most commonly sold items are the peacock "eyed" tail, the peacock sword, and stripped peacock eyes.

Peacock sword   Stripped peacock eye

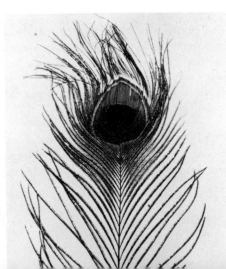

Peacock eyed tail

MARABOU. Sold prepacked in basic colors of white, red, yellow, blue, black, olive, gray, and orange, this fluffy turkey feather may be had in lengths from four to six inches. It is widely acclaimed and used by tiers because of its "breathing" action when fished.

Most of the marabou you will find will be of the long-stemmed variety, and it will be the flues coming off the stem that will be tied in as streamer wings. If, however, you can find a supplier listing marabou "blood feathers" about four inches long, buy some. "Blood feathers," or "shorts" as they are sometimes called, are the undeveloped marabou feather as it comes from the bird. All the flues lie forward toward the tip, as opposed to coming out sideways. All you have to do is lay one complete feather along the shank, and you will have perfect taper and action with less effort.

Marabou

PHEASANTS. General listings include silver, ringneck, golden, Lady Amherst, and Reeves. They are sold in entire skins, by the neck cape, paired wings, tails, and body feathers prepacked by the dozen.

Two of the more popular neck capes are the golden and the Lady Amherst, both having tippet feathers and crests. The body plumage of the silver pheasant, Reeves, and ringneck offers extensive material for various fly-tying uses.

Golden pheasant neck

Silver pheasant plumage

Reeves pheasant body feathers

Lady Amherst neck

OSTRICH. As far as I know, none of these birds are raised in the United States for the production of their plumage. These feathers are imported by the larger wholesalers and used primarily in the making of expensive frills on dresses and other garments, besides being used as decorative adornments in burlesque shows and Hollywood sets.

Ostrich of the first quality is quite expensive. If you were to import a top-grade ostrich stick it would cost you in the neighborhood of one dollar—wholesale.

The ostrich offered to the flytier are those damaged or imperfect sticks the wholesaler cannot use—or, in the case of color, if there is an overrun. Since there is a tremendous amount of volume in ostrich sales to other fields, there are quite enough leftovers for the tier. Actually, we do not need a perfect stick, only a perfect herl.

Ostrich may be bought by the pack or stick in the usual array of colors. In addition to the dyed variety, there are occasions when you will find some in natural black, brown, gray, and chinchilla. An assortment of the different shades is a welcome addition to your collection.

GUINEA HEN. Common and inexpensive. Sold prepacked in natural and dyed colors. Always a good item to have around, considering its many uses.

Ostrich plume Guinea hen plumage

TURKEY. Thank God for this bird, especially for its speckled brown wing quills that have tied so many Muddlers and Hoppers. The speckled, or mottled brown turkey wing quill is one of the most popular items sold by supply houses, along with peacock and rooster necks.

Also generally listed are dark brown turkey tails and body feathers, which can be dyed into a variety of shades. Occasionally the barred black and white, the scarce cinnamon, or gray wing quills are also listed.

The price of these feathers is still very reasonable though this may change in the future, since more and more white turkeys are being raised rather than the old-fashioned brown and gray.

Feathers are usually sold in matched pairs, or dozens.

Speckled brown turkey wing quills

Dark brown turkey tails

GOOSE. Listed in useable shades and sold in paired lefts and rights, or by the dozen, also paired. These are of course the wing quills, whether of domestic white or natural gray wild geese.

Also listed are the breast and side feathers of the domestic white. Again in all required shades.

DUCK. Domestic and some game species, especially the mallard and wood duck.

Most houses list duck pointer quills, the flank, and the breast feathers for sale in prepackaged units.

In addition to natural mallard and wood duck (if available) flank, these side feathers are also sold dyed, usually in imitation wood duck, light yellow, and pale green.

Breast feathers of the domestic white duck are sometimes listed as "fan-wing" material.

TEAL. Common listings include only the teal flank, both natural and dyed, and paired wings.

Goose wing quills   Mallard duck wings

Teal flank feathers

Depending on the catalog and the supplier's stockpile, some concerns still list skins and feathers of birds no longer available under current regulations—such as kingfisher, tetrus pheasant, and snipe. Because they were in stock prior to certain deadline dates, these materials may still be sold legitimately. If there are some of these you do not as yet have, it would be a wise move to stock up now before they become completely unavailable.

DUBBING MATERIAL

The following list is a general rundown of common furs, mostly used for dubbing, available to the tier through a materials house.

BEAVER. Excellent dubbing fur. Very water resistant as is the case with many of the water mammals. Light gray underfur and blue gray back. Takes bleaching and redyeing readily without sacrificing too much of its quality. Sold prepacked.

HARE'S MASK WITH EARS. Imported from Europe, these are larger than our cottontail or snowshoe rabbits. Has both soft and bristly fur. Excellent dubbing for fuzzy effects. Sold prepacked, either by ears alone or with entire face mask and ears.

MOLE. A complete skin is approximately four by six inches. Moles are gray in their natural state, though they may also be had in dyed brown and black. The fur is soft and makes extremely fine dubbing.

Hare's mask

Beaver

MUSKRAT. Most sold of all furs for dubbing. The natural color is medium-dark blue gray on back, medium-light blue gray on belly. Prepackaged by pieces, it may occasionally be purchased in entire skin units at bargain rates.

AUSTRALIAN OPOSSUM. Medium gray fur over most of the animal, but a yellowish cream underside, which makes this an excellent natural dubbing fur for such patterns as the Light Cahill. Prepacked.

American opossum, though a fine fur with a lifelike luster, is rarely listed, probably because of its all-white fur. A fine candidate for the dyebath.

OTTER. Light tan to dark brown. The otter provides coarse-type dubbing when its short guard hairs are mixed with the softer underfur. It is a water animal and very popular. Sold in pieces prepacked.

Muskrat   Australian opossum

Otter

RABBIT. Natural white, brown, gray, and black—also in all dyed colors. Rabbit is common and inexpensive, and it provides excellent dubbing for wet flies. Prepacked and in some cases sold by the entire skin.

Rabbit

RACCOON. Brown dubbing. Takes readily to bleaching into a creamy yellow. It is a common fur and comes prepacked.

Raccoon

SEAL. Sold prepacked on the skin in shades of brown or dyed black. Fur very soft. This and shredded coarse Greenland seal are both excellent dubbers, though the latter requires extra precautions in making it adhere to the thread.

Coarse seal fur is sold in almost every shade needed for the flytier.

TAILS AND HIDES FOR WINGING AND TAILING

BUCKTAIL. Used in streamers and saltwater flies mainly, it is listed by every materials house in both natural and dyed colors.

CALF TAIL. Common and widely used in all tying. Natural white, brown, tan, black, and all dyed colors. Sold by the tail and in bulk.

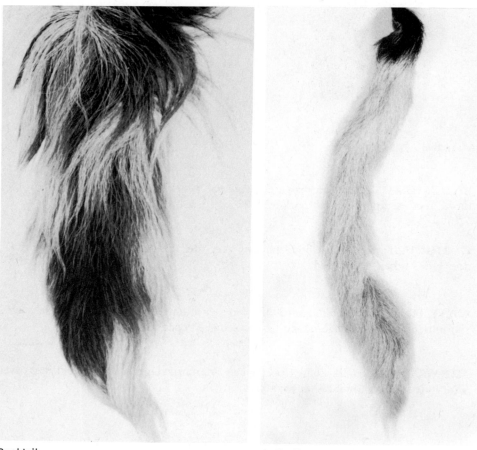

Bucktail   Calf tail

ANTELOPE. Pieces sold prepacked. The hair is coarse and brown and white in color; it flares for hair-bug tying.

FITCH. The tail is used for winging material, while the creamy yellow body hair makes excellent dubbing. It is sold prepacked and is often slightly more expensive than some other furs and hides.

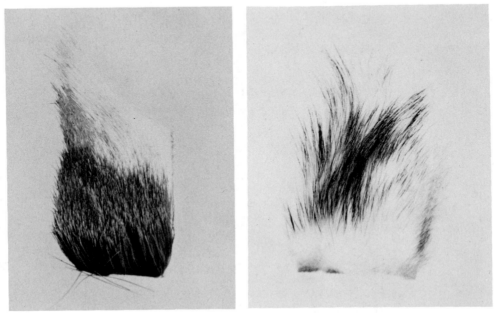

Antelope   Fitch

BLACK BEAR. This bear provides brownish black winging material; its underfur is also useable. Sold prepackaged.

CARIBOU. Tannish gray body hair of very fine texture. It is used for spinning deer-hair bodies. Prepacked.

GRAY FOX. The barred guard hairs are excellent for winging material, while the underfur is highly desirable for dubbing. Prepacked.

MOOSE MANE. This comes prepacked in natural gray and sometimes dyed. The hair is used for ribbing material.

Caribou

Black bear

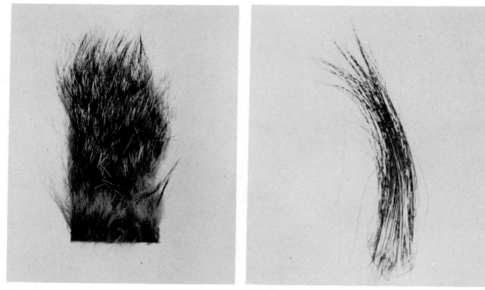

Gray fox

Moose mane

POLAR BEAR. Natural white, creamy white, and dyed into most common colors. It is slightly expensive by comparison to other hides, probably because of its diminishing availability. Prepacked.

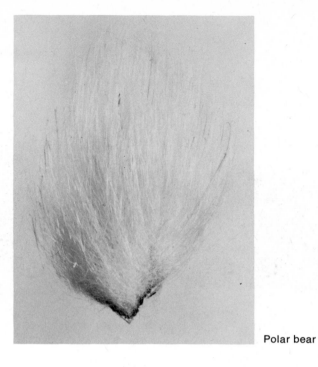

Polar bear

PORCUPINE. Prepacked. Both the quills and bristles are used for tying.

SQUIRREL TAIL. The two most commonly listed are gray and red fox, though occasionally some pine, natural black, and other scarcer varieties are offered. Squirrel tail is very popular in streamer tying.

Squirrel skin, which is an excellent dubbing material, is sold now and again by a few companies.

Squirrel tail

PECCARY. Actually a wild pig, it has stiff hairs which make for fine tailing and feeler material on nymphs. Sold prepacked.

ELK. Since this is slightly coarser and stronger than deer hair, it has come into more use recently for support in hackleless flies. Sold in natural brown and dyed shades.

Elk

Peccary

TINSELS AND WIRES

For the ribbing of streamer and wet-fly bodies, the average mail-order house will list tinsel in gold and silver only. Occasionally you will find a concern that will also include bronze and some coated in various colors.

The three basic sizes sold are numbers 10, 14, and 18. Size 10 is the largest and 18 the smallest in diameter. Veniard's, the English materials house, lists no less than eleven different sizes of flat tinsel in both gold and silver. However, the three basic sizes will more than meet the needs of most tiers. Only on rare occasions will an in-between size be essential.

Tinsels are manufactured in flat, oval, and embossed styles. The oval, also in three basic sizes, is made by winding a fine-diameter tinsel around a thread core. The embossed has on its flat surface either some dotted impressions or diagonally zigzag lines molded into it, causing a distorted light refraction when it is tied onto a pattern.

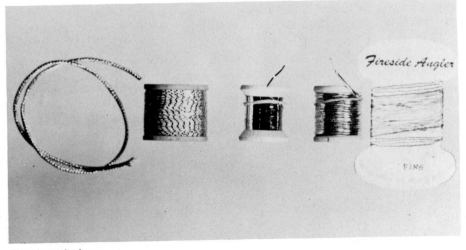

Tinsels and wires

Tinsels are usually sold on cards or spools, either in ten-yard quantities or by the ounce spool. The latter is the most economical if you do a good deal of tying.

The most important consideration you can give any tinsel is whether or not it has a protective coating (which will prevent it from tarnishing). This does not mean it will not wear or corrode after repeated use in water. It will. What you do not want, however, is the kind that will turn while it is merely sitting on your tying bench, waiting to be used.

Wires are sold in both gold and silver, with an occasional listing in copper. They will be either of the solid wire variety or, in slightly larger diameter, those having a wire-wound thread core, almost like a very fine oval tinsel.

One other wire listed is that made of solid lead. It can be had in thicknesses ranging from fine to medium to wide, and should be chosen according to the size of the pattern to be weighted.

In recent years certain synthetic tinsels have come on the market that are lighter in weight and also untarnishable. They have in many instances replaced the standard tinsel in the tying of particular patterns. Two of the most common are Mylar and Lurex. They are sold in strips, sheets, tubing, and thread forms. A specific discussion of Mylar will appear in a later chapter. These materials are a welcome addition to the tier's supply.

LACQUERS AND CEMENTS

No catalog would be complete without a listing of these much-used liquids, the foremost of which is the common head cement, or clear lacquer as it is sometimes called. Head cement is somewhat like the old airplane cement we used when building plane models as children. It's also similar to the clear nail polish women paint their fingers with, which, incidentally, you can use, should you happen to run short on your own supply of lacquer.

Lacquers, enamels, or varnishes may be had in such common colors as red, white, black, green, orange, blue, and yellow in one-ounce jars. They are intended for use in the painting of certain streamer heads, and the making of colorful cork-bodied bass bugs.

If you do not use these lacquers often enough, they have a tendency to evaporate. For this reason, besides the lacquers themselves, supply houses also sell a product called a thinner. Unless you tie a quantity of bass bugs, it is wise to check your lacquer supply now and again, and if it is getting thick and heavy, apply a little of the thinner to it. It will last much longer. An easy way to accomplish this is to use an eyedropper; fill it with some of the thinner, and then release the solution into the thickened lacquer.

Lacquers

MISCELLANEOUS MATERIALS

KAPOK. Actually a cottony fiber covering the seeds of a tropical plant, this import is used primarily in the manufacture of life preservers. If it has that kind of buoyancy, you know why it belongs on a dry fly. Color is cream. Sold prepacked. Very inexpensive.

RAFFIA. This is also a plant fiber, cultivated in Madagascar. Its toughness makes it an ideal material for the bodies of many patterns. It is sold prepacked in common colors.

Raffia

CORK. Straight cylindrical, bullet-shaped, tapered, and concave-headed, slanted and slotted are the most common offerings of the bark from the cork trees of Spain and Portugal. For fly fishermen in troutless country, or under conditions of midsummer doldrums, making and fishing the cork-bodied bass bugs has kept the action going. It is listed in all catalogs and sold prepacked by the dozens and hundreds. Sizes vary from one-eighth-inch diameter to one full inch—lengths to one-and-one-half inches.

WAXES. Usually sold in cakes of various stickiness, and so listed. The average fly-tying wax can be used without any undue residue adhering to the fingers, and is sufficient for general work in dubbing or waxing threads. When additional adhesion is required, such waxes as the Thompson Tinned wax are desirable, though you will have to clean your fingers before proceeding onto the next pattern. Listed in all materials catalogs.

FLY-TYING KITS

Most supply houses list fly-tying kits of various types, and in general they are good. What you should watch out for are those inexpensive kits that do not list exactly all the materials contained in the kit. Avoid them. Many of the kits offered in local sporting goods stores are of inferior quality, though if you judged them by the decorative carton they are contained in, you would not think so.

I believe I still have most of the materials from the first and only kit I purchased when I began tying my own flies. Most of it was fill-in waste of various sizes and colors I never found a use for.

This is the trouble with many kits today. They contain thoughtless assortments. A fly-tying kit, if it is well prepared, should provide correct materials for tying some of the known standard patterns.

I particularly recommend the Pattern Kit, originated by Fireside Angler and now sold by a few of the other materials houses. (The Orvis Company's is another.) There are approximately a dozen different kinds of these. Pattern Kits are designed for *one fly only*. Included in these kits are complete instructions for tying a particular pattern. For example, a Light Cahill Pattern Kit will have a pamphlet illustrating and telling you how to tie that pattern, all the necessary materials, excluding tools, to tie it with, and in addition have enclosed a professionally tied fly with which to compare your efforts. The actual fly is even better than a color photograph since you will see the true color *and* the proportions of the imitation.

The thought behind these Pattern Kits was that if one dry fly could be tied correctly, others in the same category would offer very few problems, since most of the basic operations would be identical.

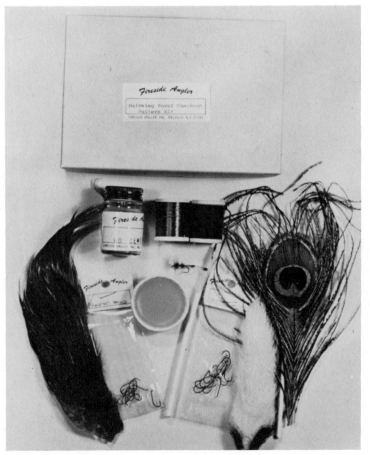

One Pattern Tying Kit

These kits are offered in dry, wet, nymph, and streamer series, in addition to some saltwater patterns. They give the beginner a proven short route, at the least expense, for getting started in fly tying. Good tools, of course, are an added necessity.

Other worthwhile kits for the novice would be those designed to tie either dry flies only, or wets, streamers, or bass bugs specifically. Materials in these would be for the purpose intended.

No kit or book, though, is as helpful as attending a fly-tying course in your locality, or working with a proficient tier. If you can do this first, the books, kits, and materials will then be more readily understood. And you'll soon be able to progress on your own.

4 Hooks

When it comes right down to it, the only thing between you and the fish is your hook.

You can spend a small fortune on rod, reel, line, vest, boots, and gadgets, not to mention travel expenses, and then blow the whole fishing trip if you skimp on an inferior quality hook. Or, for that matter, one that has not been properly sharpened.

The hook is the only item we tie our materials on to.

Though there are over ten thousand varieties, styles, and sizes of hooks being manufactured throughout the world, our concern will be only with those types that will tie our dry, wet, nymph, streamer, salmon, and saltwater flies. In this area alone there will be enough variety to give no small amount of confusion.

However, all of this complexity will be simplified by this one basic rule: *Use the proper hook for the fishing it was intended for, and tie your materials accordingly.* For each type of fly-fishing the proper hook will be discussed. Let's look at styles and size designations first.

STYLE

Hooks come in three basic shapes of bend—Model Perfect Round, Sproat, and Limerick.

For fly tying, the four most common ways the eye of the hook is formed are: up, down, looped, and ringed. These are sometimes abbreviated in the following manner:

TDE (turned-down eye)
TUE (turned-up eye)

The words looped or ringed are added if such is the case.

Hooks, depending for what purpose, or where, they are to be fished, are coated in various ways. For most freshwater fly tying and fishing the finish is bronze.

They are also made in gold-plated, japanned-black, cadmium-plated, tinned, nickel-plated, and stainless. The last four are used primarily for saltwater fly-fishing, to prevent the corrosive effects of the salt water.

The only hook that will not be affected at all by even salt water is that made of stainless steel. But a word of caution: since they will not corrode, these hooks will also not dissolve, as is the case with other hooks when they are taken by a lost fish, or one that has been released after taking the hook too deeply. Stainless steel hooks will remain with the fish indefinitely, unless the fish is jaw-hooked, in which case it may be able to rid itself of the hook by rubbing against some underwater object. If a fish is to be released it is advisable to use either a tinned or cadmium-plated hook when tying for saltwater species.

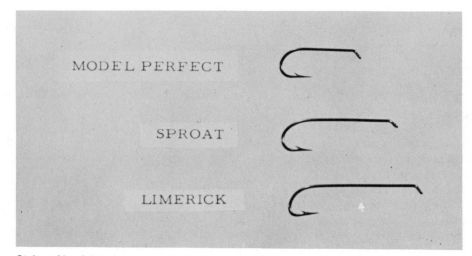

Styles of hook bend

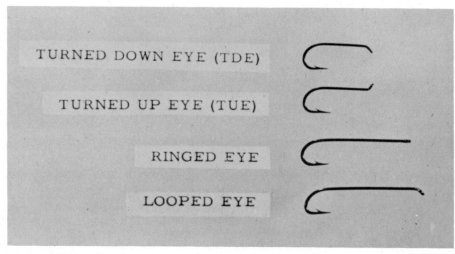

Styles of hook eyes

SIZES AND DESIGNATIONS

If you can imagine the hook size number "One" as being in the middle of the scale dividing the smaller from the larger hooks you will have no problem.

Hooks *smaller* than size one progress toward *larger* numbers in this order: 1, 2, 4, 6, 8, 10, 12, 14, 16, 18, 20, 22, 24, 26, and 28. In this group hook size 1 is the largest and size 28 the smallest.

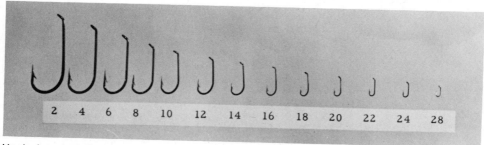

Hook sizes (small)

Progressing in the opposite direction on the scale the numbers have a zero added with a slash mark between them in this fashion: 1, 1/0, 2/0, 3/0, 4/0, 5/0, 6/0, 7/0, 8/0, 9/0 and on up to 20/0 or 30/0 for sharks, tuna, and what have you. Here the smallest hook on the scale is size one, and the largest 30/0.

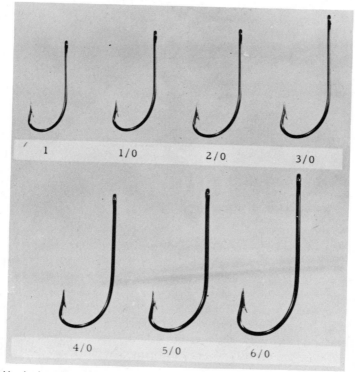

Hook sizes (large)

Hook size is determined by the width of the hook gap, not the overall length, or style of the hook.

Hook length, thickness, and fineness are different matters, and there are special designations for these also.

A hook longer than standard is designated as XL for "extra long." The degree in which it is longer is determined by the number preceding the designation. For example, let's use the Mustad hook number 3665A. This is marked 6XL on the box, which means it is one-half again as long *in shank* as that of a standard length hook. The hook gap remains the same, only the shank has been lengthened. Using this as a guide, a hook marked 3XL would only be one quarter longer than standard.

Hook shank lengths range from 1XL to 8XL.

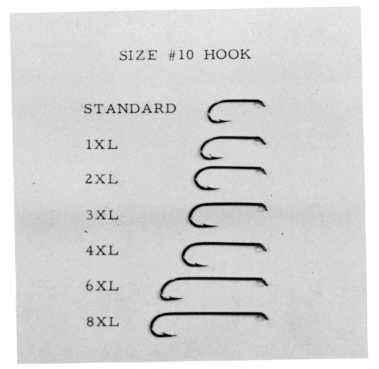

Hook shank length designations

Heavy and fine hooks are also labeled according to their classification. Thus a 3XF would be a very light wire hook. This does not mean it is three times as light in weight as a standard hook of the same size; it is just a degree of fineness to a third lighter than the standard.

A hook designated as a 2X Stout has a little more metal in it. Hooks such as these are manufactured for wet-fly or nymph fishing.

One final designation indicates the short shank hook. It is the opposite of the extra long and they are usually marked as being 1X short, or 5X short; these are used for tying spiders.

That's all there is to this little mystery.

DRY-FLY HOOKS

These are generally all fine wire hooks made from standard to superfine wire.

The important thing to remember is to use the correct hook to support the particular pattern without sacrificing strength. A superfine wire (3XF) hook will straighten more readily than that of a standard fine wire. And this happens, in most cases, when you have a good fish on the line.

For certain high-riding patterns such as hairwings, Wulffs, clipped-deer-bodied, or bushy flies, there is no need for an extrafine wire hook. If, however, you are tying sparsely hackled flies, or imitations with light, nonfloatable material, such as Cahills, Gordons, and Hendricksons, an extrafine wire hook will give you some additional buoyancy.

When you get down to the smaller sizes such as 18, 20, and 22, the standard fine wire will give you strength where it is needed, and the weight differential here is negligible. These tiny hooks almost float by themselves.

Dry-fly hooks come in both down and up eye. The up eye is recommended for the midge sizes from 20 to 28 because it gives the hook gap more clearance when striking a fish.

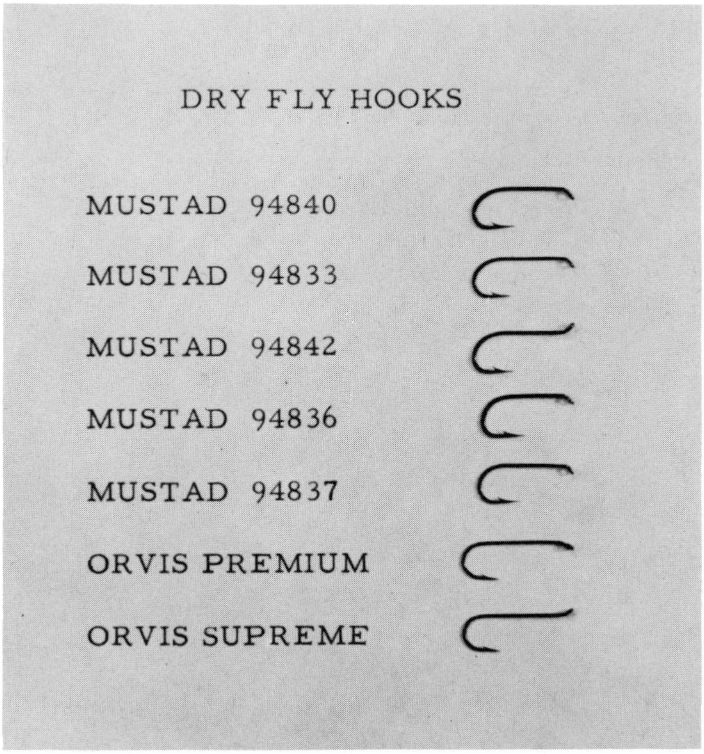

DRY FLY HOOKS

MUSTAD 94840

MUSTAD 94833

MUSTAD 94842

MUSTAD 94836

MUSTAD 94837

ORVIS PREMIUM

ORVIS SUPREME

Dry fly hooks

Some of the more popular hooks used in dry-fly tying are:

Mustad 94840—TDE, M.P. bend, fine wire
Mustad 94833—TDE, M.P. bend, 3XF wire

Mustad 94842—TUE, M.P. bend, fine wire
Mustad 94836—TDE, M.P. bend, fine wire, 1X short
Mustad 94837—TDE, M.P. bend, 3XF wire, 1X short
Orvis Premium—TDE, M.P. bend, 3XF wire, 1XL
Orvis Supreme—TUE, M.P. bend, 4XF wire, 1XL

There are, of course, many others in the dry-fly category. All of the pertinent data regarding them will be listed by the supplier in his catalog.

One other dry-fly hook you may be interested in is the Mustad 94845, which is the same as the 94840, except that it is barbless. This is an ideal hook, especially in the smaller sizes, if fish are to be released.

WET-FLY AND NYMPH HOOKS

Both wet and nymph hooks are basically in the same category. They are manufactured of heavier-gauge wire in order to sink the fly. Generally the nymph hook is a little longer in shank length than the standard wet-fly variety.

Common wet-fly hooks are:

Mustad 3906—TDE, Sproat bend, heavy wire
Mustad 3906B—TDE, Sproat bend, heavy wire, 1XL
Mustad 9671—TDE, M.P. bend, heavy wire, 2XL
Mustad 3908—TDE, Sproat bend, extraheavy wire
Mustad 7948A—TDE, M.P. bend, extraheavy wire

Common nymph hooks are:

Mustad 3906B—TDE, Sproat bend, heavy wire, 1XL
Mustad 9671—TDE, M.P. bend, heavy wire, 2XL
Mustad 9672—TDE, M.P. bend, 3XL

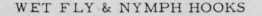

WET FLY & NYMPH HOOKS

MUSTAD 3906

MUSTAD 3906B

MUSTAD 9671

MUSTAD 3908

MUSTAD 7948A

MUSTAD 9672

Wet fly and nymph hooks

STREAMER AND BUCKTAIL HOOKS

Since both streamer and bucktail flies are primarily designed to imitate bait-fish of various sizes, the hooks are mostly of the long-shanked variety, though standard in weight.

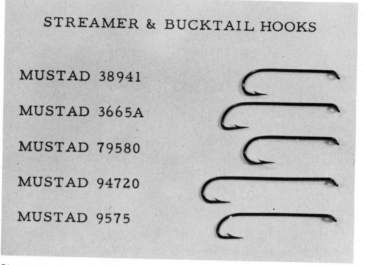

STREAMER & BUCKTAIL HOOKS

MUSTAD 38941

MUSTAD 3665A

MUSTAD 79580

MUSTAD 94720

MUSTAD 9575

Streamer and bucktail hooks

Streamers for high water, springwater, or lakes are usually weighted with fine lead wire if the intent is to get them down deep.

Popular streamer and bucktail hooks are:

Mustad 38941—TDE, Sproat bend, 3XL
Mustad 3665A—TDE, Limerick bend, 6XL
Mustad 79580—TDE, M.P. bend, 4XL
Mustad 94720—TDE, M.P. bend, 8XL
Mustad 9575—Looped TDE, Limerick bend, 6XL

The Mustad 9575 has a loop eye. Anytime you can tie with a hook of this sort, without sacrificing the pattern, do so. The looped eye is formed by extending the wire from the shank back around and alongside of it, thereby leaving no cutting edges as in other hooks with a normal closed eye. This type of finish will save many a leader from parting.

Standard hooks, without the looped eye, should always be carefully closed, where the shank ends at the eye, with tying thread; this saves the leader from slipping out or fraying.

SALMON HOOKS

If you mixed one hundred assorted styles of hooks in a box, you would have no problem in picking out the one salmon hook thrown in. It is the only one that will be black (japanned). It will also have a looped-up eye, whether it is for dry, wet, or a double hook.

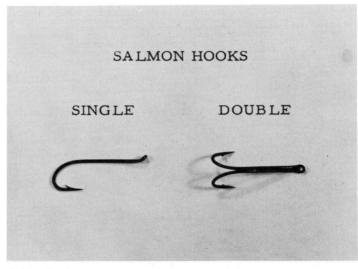

Salmon hooks

Salmon hooks come in light wire for dry flies, such as the Mustad 90240, standard wire for wets, such as the 36890, also Mustad, or in doubles usually of English manufacture. Doubles are twin hooks having separate shanks which are welded together, the entire hook manufactured from one piece of wire. The front of the shank bends around, remaining open at that position, thus forming the loop eye.

Excellent salmon hooks may be obtained from the English fly-tying firm, E. Veniard, Ltd. They carry all styles in both singles and doubles.

SALTWATER HOOKS

Fly tying for salt water is, by comparison, still in its infancy. Known and recognized patterns are few, though this art is gathering momentum yearly.

Some of the hooks used in tying for these species are the following:

> Mustad 3407—tinned, ringed eye, Sproat bend
> Mustad 3408B—tinned, down eye, Sproat bend
> Mustad 34007—stainless, ringed eye, Sproat bend
> Mustad 3489—tinned, TDE, Sproat bend, extralong shank
> Mustad 9082A—nickel-plated, long shank, right-angle kink for poppers, open soft ring

Effective fly-casting limits hook sizes to 3/0. After that the weight of the hook outbalances the line.

Though the above hooks are especially designed for salt water in that they are tinned, nickel-plated, or stainless steel, bronzed freshwater hooks also serve for such use. Freshwater hooks will not last as long, but in many cases they are perfectly made for a particular species.

Does it really matter if you can use them only for a trip or two? If a pattern has taken a fish, it has been worth the tying. Consider how many Cahills and Gordons are lost in trees, or snubbed off on submerged logs. Why then worry over the loss of one fly tied for the salt, especially since these patterns are easier to tie in the first place?

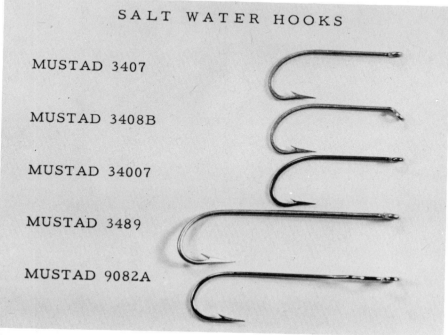

Saltwater hooks

HOOKS FOR BASS AND PANFISH

Most of the hooks used for wets, nymphs, and streamers can also be used for bass and a variety of panfish. Size is the only factor involved here, depending upon whether you are tying a streamer imitation or a deer-hair frog or mouse.

Kinked hooks for poppers

However, when it comes to tying poppers, you will need a hook designed to stay put in the cork body. For this reason there are kinked, or hump-shanked hooks.

Some of the popular kinked-shank hooks are:

Mustad 33900—ringed eye, kinked, Sproat bend
Mustad 33903—ringed eye, extralong shank, Sproat bend, kinked double
Mustad 33904ST—ringed eye, cadmium-plated and tinned, extralong shank, special kink

One little tip you might remember when tying poppers is to wind some tying thread onto the kinked portion of the hook shank before gluing and inserting it into the cork popper body. This will help prevent slippage and rotation.

The foregoing are some of the better hooks being manufactured. The very best hook, however, will lose fish if it is not kept to as sharp a point as possible.

Before tying any pattern, sharpen the point of each hook with either an Arkansas knife blade or pencil-point file. It takes very little time to give it an edge. You can at this time also check to see if the particular hook is faulty in any way. If it is, discard it. Most hooks are inexpensive. It's better to cry over a lost hook than a lost fish.

5 Tools

Though not considered materials as such, tools are the foundation for every flytier. The difference between success and failure is often a matter of quality tools, precision manufactured, to serve their proper and respective uses. I therefore would not wish to omit the few necessary basics, as well as some of the offbeat devices that I have found useful in my own tying.

The tools you cannot do without are few—vise, hackle pliers, tweezers, dubbing needle, and a bobbin. I strongly urge you to *buy the highest quality tools available*. I am not referring to cost, but generally you only get what you pay for, and the less expensive tools will usually not hold up as well as the more costly ones. Well-manufactured tools should last you a lifetime.

THE VISE. After having tried approximately a dozen different types of vises, I still tie 90 percent of my patterns with the Thompson Model "A." Its scope is almost complete, with such exceptions as trying to tie the larger saltwater flies, or having a rotary feature, neither of which is needed by most trout fishermen. This vise is extremely well made, is height and angle adjustable, and will hold hooks from sizes 1/0 to 28 with no difficulty. I even prefer this over Thompson's "Ultra" Vise, which features an adjustable collet angle and therefore costs a few dollars more. The angle on the model "A" is just perfect, while the adjustable one has a habit of slipping now and again.

The Thompson Model "B" vise, while having excellent jaws for the gripping of the same range of hooks, is not adjustable to height, which can be a disadvantage, depending on the size of your tying table. It also opens and closes its jaws by means of a rotating knob, as opposed to the more convenient lever used in the Model "A."

Two other vises I find use for on occasion are those made by Veniard's in England. One is the Salmo Vise, again a well-precisioned tool which, while it will take all the smaller-sized hooks, has additional gap expansion to allow the fitting of some of the saltwater variety, up to size 6/0, to be grasped within its jaws. This vise is also knob-screw operated, as opposed to the lever action, but overcomes this disadvantage by being height adjustable, angle settable, and in addition has a 360° rotary feature. The diameters of the stems of the Thompson Model "A" and the Salmo are very close, and it is therefore possible to interchange them easily, depending on your intended use, without removing the base, which may be permanently clamped to your tying table.

The other vise manufactured by this English firm is an affair called the "Croydon" hand vise. And that is exactly what it is. This device has, although very well made, simple chuck jaws, enabling the tier to fasten hooks within them from sizes 6 to 22. It is primarily intended for use afield. It will fit into your left palm very comfortably, and will give you that "third" hand, when trying to tie flies the hard way.

There are, of course, many other vises on the market, some of which are quite good. One vise I do not use, yet which may interest you, is that made by the Universal Vise Company. It is called the Universal Rotary Vise, and its main feature is that you can completely revolve the barrel, or head, in a continuous motion should you desire, or have a need to do so. One need would be winding onto the hook shank a length of tinsel by simply tying in the latter, holding on to it and rotating the vise with the large disc placed at its aft end for the purpose. In principle, this vise has ideal uses; but I wish its manufacturer would use a more durable steel and finish it in appearance and precision. It does not meet its full potential. If it did, I would be willing to pay a few dollars extra for the quality product.

HACKLE PLIERS. The purpose of this tool is to be able to wind the hackles of a feather around the shank of a hook. It should be able to do so without cutting the hackle, or slipping off while the hackle is being wound. The best pair of hackle pliers I have ever used were those originated by the late Herb Howard who, very fortunately for all tiers, sold his rights to the pliers to a manufacturer, prior to his death. These pliers are today sold by most of the materials houses, some of which carry his name in advertising the product.

For exceptionally fine work, especially on hooks in sizes 20 and smaller, I prefer the small hackle pliers made by Veniard's in England. They are very light, hold the hackle well without cutting, and therefore make for a less frustrating operation in the tying of midges.

SCISSORS. For the flytier the ideal pair of scissors should have well-meshing blades, tapering to as fine a point as possible, with finger holes of adequate size for the individual tier. Many firms make such precision tools, though not specifically for the flytier. Some of the best I have used were either of a Wiss or Solingen manufacture.

Besides these two firms, I have just recently acquired a pair of Iris Scissors which, though they have rather small finger holes, are excellently tapered to an almost needlelike point, ideally suited for the trimming of hackle in close quarters.

Besides obtaining the fine and delicately pointed pair, you should also acquire another pair of scissors of the heavy-duty type, to be used for the cutting of tinsel and other hard materials. Do not overburden fine scissors with work that was not intended for them.

TWEEZERS. Here again, the key feature of a good pair of tweezers is a needlelike point that can get into the remote corners of a hackle for plucking unwanted or stray fibers. There are many varieties of these on the market; one of the best places to look for them, other than a materials house, is a surgical supply firm. If the tweezers you own are of fair to good quality, you can further improve their usefulness by filing them down, tapering them to as fine a point as possible, without losing their gripping power. The pair I use is of Swiss manufacture, made of stainless steel, with points so fine, were you to drop them, they would imbed themselves in a wooden floor.

DUBBING NEEDLE (or BODKIN). This is a simple, yet indispensable tool, which consists of a straight needle imbedded in wood or plastic. Besides its usefulness in plucking fur or hairs, it is also utilized for the application of head lacquer to the finished fly, or doubling a wing case on a nymph pattern. All supply houses carry this item, and most are as good as any other for their various purposes. They are inexpensive enough, but if you wish to take the time you can make your own by inserting a large-sized sewing needle into a piece of plastic or wood. A dab of epoxy at the juncture will secure it.

BOBBIN. While some tiers never use these thread holders, I find one a necessity. The fingers of my hand tend to be on the rough side and have a habit of fraying any thread of fine diameter. Using a bobbin, my hands will not have to touch the thread until the final whip finish, in addition to making the operations on the various patterns neater and faster.

I also use a bobbin for winding a tapered floss body. Try it sometime.

Two bobbins I recommend are the Chase Bobbin and the S & M Bobbin. I have found the latter to be superior to all that I have tried. It is a simple affair, made of stainless steel, which will hold a standard-sized spool of thread. Tension on this bobbin is set by applying finger pressure, either outward or inward, along the sides of this tool. There is no difficulty in use should you insert a size 8/o thread into it. Since this particular bobbin is hand-beveled at each end of the tube for smoothness, it will not cut thread as some of the machine-manufactured ones will.

The foregoing are the basic necessities you will require. There are, however, certain other tools and gadgets all flytiers accumulate to make fly tying more pleasant. A few that you may also find use for are:

MATERIAL CLIP. This is a small device that clamps onto the barrel of a standard vise. Made of spring steel, the upper portion will separate and hold stray material out of the way, while other operations are being performed on the particular pattern. When not in use, it can be rotated to the underside of the barrel and so be out of the way.

HACKLE GAUGE. Though I do not use one myself, this gadget would be of some help for the beginning flytier in the development of a sense of proportion concerning hackle size. Its traverse lines indicate the radius of the hackle feather size for the relative hook.

HACKLE GUARDS. These are small discs that are placed over the eye of the hook on a finished fly to keep the hackle out of the way when tying the whip finish on the completed fly. Again, an excellent tool for the novice.

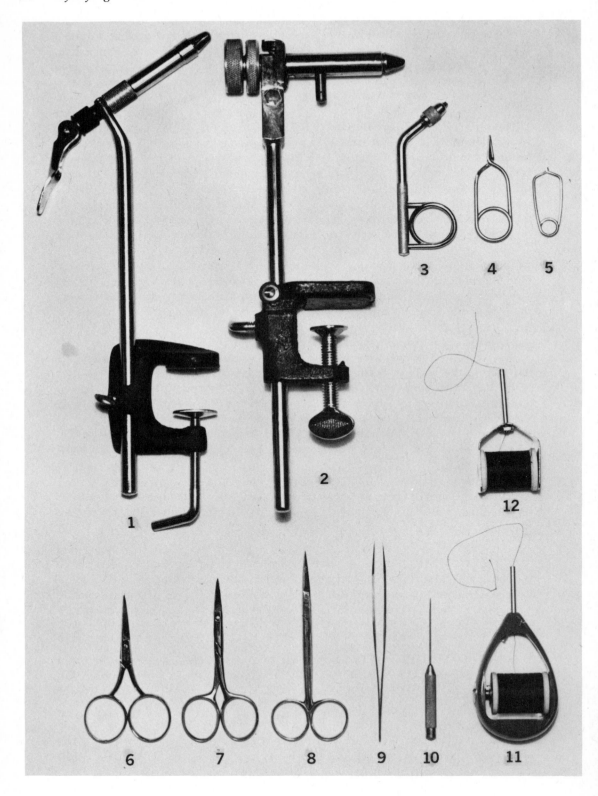

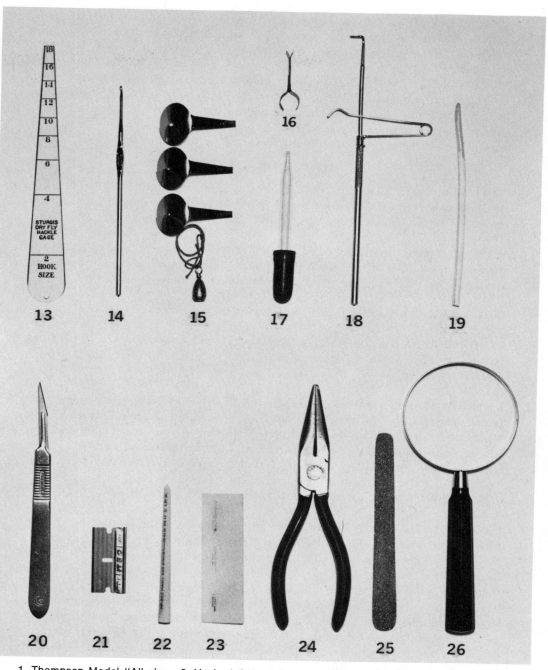

1. Thompson Model "A" vise   2. Veniard Salmo vise   3. Veniard Croydon hand vise
4. Herb Howard hackle pliers   5. Small Veniard pliers   6. Solingen straight-blade scissors   7. Wiss curved-blade scissors   8. Iris scissors   9. Swiss needlepoint tweezers
10. Dubbing needle   11. Chase bobbin   12. S & M bobbin   13. Sturgis hackle gauge
14. Crochet needle   15. Hackle guard set   16. Material clip   17. Eyedropper   18.
Whip finisher   19. Peacock butt half-hitch tool   20. Scalpel   21. Razor blade   22.
Arkansas point file   23. Arkansas knife blade file   24. Flat-nosed pliers   25. Emery
board   26. Magnifying glass

WHIP FINISHER. This tool is designed to tie the whip finish for you. It is used by quite a few professional tiers, since it completes the head on an imitation much faster than if this were done by hand.

FLAT-NOSED PLIERS. You can buy these in a hardware store. Preferably get those with narrow tips and unserrated jaws. If you cannot find them in this condition, they can be filed down. They are used for flattening lead-centered nymphs, over which floss or wool has been tied. This procedure will give a more natural appearance to the imitation being tied. Naturally, the pliers will have various other uses as well.

NAIL FILE or **EMERY BOARD.** Borrow a used one from your wife! I use one mainly to keep my fingernails and hands as smooth as possible, since, as I explained earlier, I have a habit of fraying threads and flosses.

RAZOR BLADE. Single edged, naturally. Or, if you prefer, you can go to a surgical supply firm and buy a scalpel holder and a set of insertable blades of various types. Uses for these simple instruments are endless.

MAGNIFYING GLASS. No explanation needed.

EYEDROPPER. I believe the last one I purchased cost ten cents. It provides one of the easiest vehicles I know of for transferring some thinner into a lacquer that has hardened.

KNIFE BLADE and POINT FILE SHARPENING STONES. I recommend the hard Arkansas stones for these. It is much easier to sharpen a hook prior to tying a pattern than after it has been completed. Do this at your tying table and you will decrease the number of missed strikes and lost fish astream. The knife blade file, in addition to honing the points of hooks, may also be used to give an edge to a pair of scissors or tweezers, or other similar fine tools.
   The point file stone is used mainly on smaller hooks.

CROCHET HOOK or NEEDLE. Have you ever tried to dub seal or polar bear fur? It's like trying to spin glass onto the thread. This problem may be overcome by forming a double loop in your tying thread, extending approximately five or six inches out from the hook shank, and tying it in securely where it leaves the shank. Keep the loop separated and apply some heavy head lacquer to the sides of the looped thread. Place and spread the seal fur, if this is what you are using, so that it adheres to the thread. Place the hook of the crochet needle into the end of the loop and allow the loop to close. If the seal fur is not properly aligned, this is the time to do it. Trapped between the two strands of thread, it can be moved up or down for uniformity and taper. Holding the thread taut with the crochet needle, revolve the latter with your fingers, thus twisting the thread and fur into a rope. When you have attained the security needed, grasp the twisted loop above the crochet needle with your hackle pliers, keeping tension on the thread, and wind the "rope" around the hook shank, forming the body of the fly. For this type of dubbing, I have found a crochet hook indispensable.

HALF-HITCH TOOL. Even if you utilize the half hitch in your tying, you do not have to buy this particular product. All you need is the base end of a peacock, goose, or similar quill. A section of about four inches will suffice. You will notice that the butt ends of such quills have an indentation. These will fit perfectly over the eye of the hook, and the smoothness of the quill stem will allow the half-hitch procedure to flow without effort.

TOOTHPICK. I keep a few of these imbedded in the foam plastic "steps" that sit on my fly-tying table. I use them in place of the dubbing needle where a heavy coat of head lacquer is required, in order to keep that tool from becoming unnecessarily coated and thus needing a scraping now and then.

My primary use for it, however, is the painting of the larger eye portion of an "eyed" streamer with a center pupil. By dipping the toothpick into enamel of the proper density, a small droplet forms at the point. This is then applied as the "eye," and it forms a more perfect circle or oval than if you painted it. For the pupil I then use the finer-pointed dubbing needle, and repeat the same procedure, of course after the larger "eye" has dried.

These are but a few of the tools, gadgets, and gimmicks used by various tiers, many of which are homemade. It is always a good idea to be on the lookout for any of these devices that will make the tying of flies a bit simpler and more interesting.

6 Skinning and Cleaning

Of all of the procedures connected with gathering your own fly-tying materials, skinning and cleaning are the least enjoyable. And yet they are not difficult to master, once you have done a bird or two and a few animal skins. For the uninitiated the first attempts may seem crude, but as with your fly tying, you will gain speed and dexterity with experience, and you will also have the satisfaction of knowing the work has been properly done.

Let's cover a few specimens in this chapter, and with the photographic descriptions, you will be able to perform the operation on any other species. Some may have a variable factor in that they are thicker skinned, or the hide may have certain peculiarities; some will be tougher, but for the most part relatively easy.

Virtually all animals you do flesh-out will be already dead, with the possible exception of any live domestic you may have purchased with the intention of doing your own slaughtering. If this is the case, and your bird happens to be a prime well-marked rooster, be advised that poultry farmers do not kill any chicken unless it has been starved for at least fifteen hours. This is done so that there will not be any food left in the crop, which makes for a cleaner bird, especially if you wish to have the meat for the table.

Kill a chicken as humanely as possible. The swiftest method I have found, which kills the bird instantly, is to use the flat, back end of a hatchet and give the bird a sharp rap at the juncture where the head meets the neck in back. This will break the neck cleanly. The bird will flop around a bit, as all chickens do, even when their heads are entirely cut off. Don't let this worry you. The bird is dead. While he is flopping, however, hold him head down in a disposable carton so that the blood drips into the container and not on the feathers, which you are out to protect. It is all over within minutes, and then time to skin-out your rooster.

SKINNING A ROOSTER

Take a sharp, thin-bladed knife and make an incision in the breast area just below the cape of the bird. The point of the knife should only penetrate the skin and not go into the meat. The feathers will seem to get in the way, but it is simple enough to push them aside to see what you are doing. Once you have ascertained that the knife blade has penetrated properly, run it up, blade facing you, along the underside of the skin, to the base of the head. When you become adept at this it will take about fifteen seconds for this incision to be completed. You can now take hold of the skin on either side of the opened cut and, with the aid of your knife, peel it partway from the flesh.

By now you should have a good view of your operation and also know whether or not you are going to get the whole cape out in one piece. If it looks as if you might cut it too short, just lengthen the basic cut downward a little more.

Though you can literally skin the whole bird out in one piece, I prefer to do it in parts, and keep the cape, saddle, wings, and tail separate.

If all appears in order, proceed to make a circular cut around the base, and from the underside, of the part that is holding the cape. After this incision you simply peel the cape skin off the bird by pulling it upward toward the head of the bird. Make sure you go all the way. Don't miss those small hackles. When you have peeled the cape to the head, cut it away and lay it aside. At this time, also cut the head completely off the bird.

Next remove the wings by shearing them off with a pair of garden pruners. Make sure you cut the wings so you retain the stiff feathers on the shoulder.

Having freed the wings from the rooster you can now more easily remove the saddle, which is the very back of the bird, having at its edges those long saddle feathers so often used in streamer flies. At the point where the wings and cape were removed, grasp the fold of skin at the forward part of the saddle and make your incision, freeing it and working around to each side of the portion containing the saddle. Once you have part of one side peeled away, it is only a matter of a little pulling and slicing to separate it from the bird.

All you have left now are the body feathers and the tail. The latter may just be clipped off with the pruning shears as a unit, or the feathers individually plucked from the bird. These will be useable.

I sometimes keep the body feathers, and sometimes not, depending on their shade and quality. They are not unlike the feathers you obtain from a hen neck. One of the birds I skinned recently had a very nice shade of dark blue dun gray, and I therefore saved that for winging material to be used on hackleless flies. These also can be left on the skin or plucked. Store them separately.

When you've finished skinning out your rooster, fillet the meat, wash it, and store it in your freezer for future use at the dinner table. Your next step will be to protect the neck and saddle capes you have just removed from the bird, along with the wings and tail if you have kept them.

Most birds and animals are infested with lice, fleas, or other parasites. You will not have to check too thoroughly to know if they are present. They will announce themselves shortly after the chicken has been killed. If you discover some form of life crawling on your hard-earned cape and saddle, you can immediately wash out all the skinned portions in a mild detergent, which will simultaneously clean the hackles for you; then put them on a newspaper to dry, skin side down.

Some tiers prefer to add a little borax, or borax and salt mixture, on the skin side of their capes and leave it there until dry. When using this procedure, first tack the cape to a board to spread it, to prevent shrinkage while the skin dries. All this is not absolutely essential in the case of the common chicken.

One of the best methods is simply to let the skin adhere to the newspaper it has been pressed against, and allow the latter to remain on the skin after it has dried for an indefinite period. Some capes still have remnants of newspaper on the skin long after the neck has outgrown any further usefulness.

You probably will have to wash the feathered skins, and after this they will appear to be in desperate straits—bedraggled, misshapen, and almost irreparable. Let me assure you that once the drying process starts, which should be helped along by now and again fluffing the hackles in a dry room, they will come back to better than normal and look very beautiful. However, because you have washed it, and also because of the inherent moisture remaining in the skin itself, your cape may start to curl as the moisture evaporates. When this happens, lay the cape skin down on a used magazine or newspaper, and place other such material over and on top of it. This will retain the shape of the cape for you. Since this process is started while the skin is still slightly damp, it is best to remove the skin after a day and allow it to dry out fully, after which it should again be pressed for a more permanent set.

The completely dried cape should not be flat as a pancake, but almost so, with only a slight downward curvature, feathers facing you, making for a natural appearance and, more essentially, easier picking when the cape is put to use.

During the pressing process, should some of the hackles accidentally lie awry and come out bent or twisted, the matter is resolved by using steam from the tea-kettle. Steam, if concentrated, will bring back to original shape any feathers from any birds, provided they are not overly dirty or begrimed. With fairly clean birds there is never a problem.

Quail Bantam rooster

Making incision into lower front neck area
of breast

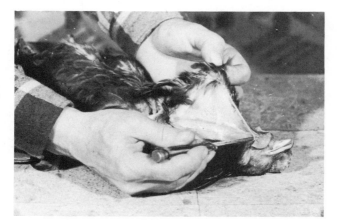

Cutting neck skin from base to beak

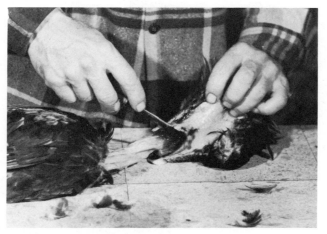

Peeling neck skin from rooster

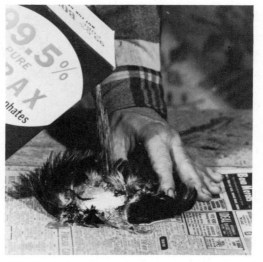

Pouring preservative of borax onto freed
neck skin

Clipping wings from rooster

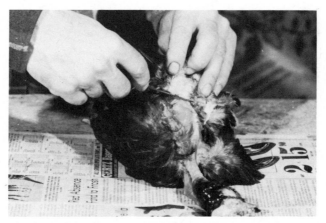

Starting incision for removal of saddle skin

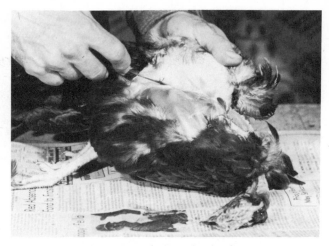

Working and freeing saddle from back of rooster

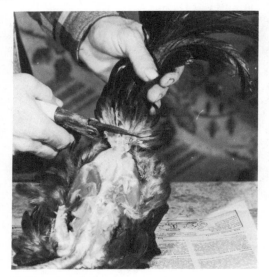

Cutting away tail section

Skinned-out neck and saddle skins

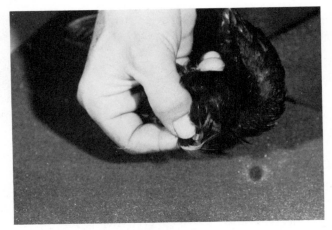

Quill fibers from wing shoulder

Stripped tail feather. Note segmentation

SKINNING A DUCK

Skinning a chicken is comparable to tying a streamer fly; for the novice it is the easiest to master in its category. Ducks will perhaps prove one of the most difficult birds to skin, and present several problems that do not exist with other members of the bird family.

Assuming you have taken a duck during gunning season, or a friend has brought you a mature, prime, drake mallard, you are faced only with the problem of skinning it out.

Lay the duck on his back and begin by inserting the point of your knife blade into the breast, just penetrating the skin. On a duck you will have to push a few more feathers aside to see what you are doing since he comes a bit more clothed, and also has a very downy undercoat, to protect him from the cold. Having located the epidermis proper, commence cutting, with the knife blade facing you, upward along the breast, into the neck, and all the way to the bill of the bird.

Now turn the duck around and extend this cutting line down to the anus, but do not penetrate it. Your incision should be a straight line the entire underside length of the duck from the bill to the base of the tail.

Proceeding, as with the rooster, slip the point of the knife under the fold of the skin on either side of the initial cut and, by slicing and pulling, carefully separate the skin from the flesh. Once you have it started the task progresses with increasing rapidity. Try to peel off as much of the skin as you can before beginning the work around the feet and the wings. When you have accomplished as much as you feel can be done in this area, you will next have to free the legs from the skin of the duck.

I have found that if I make a small cut on the inside of each leg, and peel the upper portion of this extremity, I can grasp the foot and push it through the skin till the lowest joint having feathers is exposed. I clip the joint with my pruning shears, and cut the sinews, freeing the thigh from the lower leg. This is repeated with the other foot and leg also. Now I have a bit more room to try to separate the skin at the lower back of the duck.

This particular operation is the trickiest, since the skin on a duck lies almost on the bone at this junction. Be careful and work slowly, if you do not wish to puncture the skin. If you should penetrate the skin, the damage will be small and not much is lost. But it will become a matter of pride to perform this procedure correctly, even though we are only flytiers, and not surgeons.

When working around the back of the bird, try using a sharp, thin knife and letting the blade hug the backbone, not the skin. As soon as you have been able to penetrate so that the point of the blade extends through to the other side you've been working alternately with, this task becomes a little simpler. Keep working the skin away from the backbone, and toward the base of the tail. When you reach the tail, make a cut that will separate the tail feathers as a unit, but without cutting into the anus. You'll know when you've done it correctly, and if not the first time, you will have been educated for the second attempt on another duck. In any event there is not too much lost if the wrong cut is made, since the feathers can easily be cleaned off with a damp rag.

Once you have gotten this far, the rest of the duck is not too difficult. Reverse the bird again, and start working along the back section, freeing the skin, till you reach the wings. Here, as with the legs, try peeling the skin up to the first joint after the one connecting it to the body, using your knife as an assist only. Upon reaching that joint, shear it off with the pruners. Do the same with the remaining wing.

Having freed the wings, the skin will almost pull itself off all the way to the bill. You'll have to help, of course. When you reach the head of the duck, skin past the skull and eyes and clip away the body. You now have one whole, or nearly so, duck skin. As before, fillet out the breast meat, cut off the thighs, clean, and place in the freezer.

Ducks are endowed by nature with properties that permit them to sit in water so cold that, were you to put your arm in next to them, it would come out extremely numb in a matter of seconds. Besides the heavy plumage and down, the skins of such birds as ducks and geese are fairly thick, and to the tier's dismay, extremely fatty. The amount of fat on a given duck depends on the species. Some of the diver ducks have more than those of the puddle variety, since they must withstand colder temperatures, because of their later arrival along the migratory routes.

After you have skinned-out your entire duck, your next task will be to try to remove as much as possible of the excess fat adhering to the skin. It may take more than one working over to attain a skin relatively free of fat. Usually when I do a duck skin, I will scrape as much of this fatty tissue away as I can immediately after the skinning process. I will then sprinkle a liberal amount of pure salt on it, covering all the exposed parts, but avoiding the feathers. The salt will break down the remaining tissue of fat within a day or so, and I can then do a bit more scraping. If you can repeat this procedure two or three times, you will get closer to the real skin with each scraping.

Should grease and salt get on the feathers during the scraping operation, it will cause them to mat. This can be rectified by using a damp rag and rubbing the matted area. If they dry in the matted state, it is advisable to use the steam from the teakettle. Most tiers get their ducks as clean as possible and at the last stage sprinkle some borax—the white pure kind—on the skin and let the duck dry out. Borax, besides being a cleansing chemical, also has some of the properties that are used for tanning.

All operations, whether for birds or animals, should be performed in a dry area that is free from flies, beetles, or other pests. If the skin has been salted or boraxed these vermin will not be able to lay their eggs on it. Any eggs that may have been deposited prior to the salting will not hatch if this precaution has been taken, because of the chemical properties of salt or borax. Be as careful as possible to protect your investment.

Once you have skinned both a chicken and a duck, most other birds will be relatively simple. Unless they are waterfowl, they will not have to be salted, though you can use a little borax if you wish to play it safe. This applies especially to the joint areas where the wings are attached, since you will not be able to remove all the meat and tissue from these parts. An extra application of borax at these points is advisable.

Most of the birds you obtain will have a fairly thin skin, which will peel very easily. Some are in fact a little delicate, so you will have to be a bit more careful not to tear the skin.

If your bird, whatever it may be, has completely dried, you should protect him till he is ready for use, by enclosing him in an appropriately sized poly bag, and sealing it securely by twisting the folded open ends, and wrapping the section with either a rubber band, or one of those paper-coated metal twisters used to seal in a loaf of bread. It won't do any harm if you add a small dose of paradichlorobenzene crystals to keep your bird skin company—as an added precaution in the remote chance a foreign parasite has eluded you and is enclosed in the poly bag with the bird. The addition of the crystals will serve also to help extract any excess moisture from the skin and prevent mildew. This fungus will occur if you seal an undried bird in a container where air cannot get in. If the bird is fully dry, and has been properly processed, he will last indefinitely in storage.

SKINNING ANIMALS

Furs, hides, and tails of domestic or game animals may be obtained in the raw or tanned state. Since we are dealing here with the processes of preparation of raw furs, the matter of the tanned variety will not concern us except for a brief distinction of qualities between the two.

There is one advantage of tanned fur over untanned—besides looking more attractive—and that is that it is not bothered by parasites such as the larvae of beetles and various other insects. Since all edible matter has been removed from the hide during tanning, and the skin so broken down to obtain the softness of leather, these vermin are no longer interested. The only pests that do inhabit a tanned fur are moths, which, if given a chance to take up residence, lay their eggs in it; their progeny will nourish on the fur, as they would on wool or feathers.

On the other hand, the one advantage of untanned fur over tanned is that for the flytier the fur or hide used for tailing is more desirable since it has not lost any of its properties. A tanned fur, while beautiful to look at, has had its skin rubbed a good deal during the tanning process. Most of its natural oils have been removed, the hair brushed and combed, and it is like a woman who has gone to the beauty parlor and hair stylist for the "works." She comes out looking lovely, and she is completely unconcerned that her hair has actually been damaged in the process. While I dare not press the analogy, and had in fact better praise the improvement, flytiers will look askance at certain pieces of tanned fur that have lost either a natural wild luster in a piece intended for dubbing, or in materials needed for tailing; they will be quite disturbed to find some of the ends not tapering evenly, or to a natural point.

You can, if you wish, do your own tanning. It is relatively simple. The skin of the animal must be scraped completely free of all flesh and fat, then immersed in a solution of salt and alum for a period of three to ten days, depending on the type of skin to be tanned; after removal, it should be allowed to become almost dry, yet remain damp enough to allow rubbing the skin over a wooden, axe-shaped yet blunted stake to break down the fibers in the hide. After it has been made as soft as one of your felt jackets, or nearly so, a bit of natural animal oil is reapplied to the skin to replace the oils the tanning process has originally removed. This will insure additional softness.

I was at one time intrigued by the various methods of tanning. One of the finest methods I know of is the smoking process, attributed to the Crow Indians. Most leather, upon becoming wet, gets stiff, and has to be relubricated, either with saddle soap or neat's-foot oil, and the like. The buckskin garments worn by the Crows, after having been drenched in rain or snow, dried soft, and it is believed that this was due to the smoking process they used for tanning.

Tanning can be fun, and if you have more than enough of a certain type of animal skin, by all means try it. Your finished product will make a nice addition to the wall of your den.

I have selected the woodchuck or common groundhog as our example for the process of skinning an animal because we are already familiar with him, and also because he is in the medium-sized range.

If you have done your own hunting, you will have to field-dress your animal, whether it is a woodchuck or any other game. The procedures remain the same, only the dimensions vary. The whole idea is to bleed the animal, cool the carcass, and protect it. If our 'chuck has been properly field-dressed, all that remains is the skinning and preserving.

Lay the 'chuck flat on his back on your workbench or table, and with a sharp and pointed knife make an incision beginning at the open cavity up along the inside of each hind leg. Grasp the folds of the skin that have been freed and, working with your blade, pull and peel the skin from the legs down to the foot. As you progress, work the skin away from the outer part of the thigh and lower back until you can push your hand through from one side to the other.

On the woodchuck I usually cut the tail off first, and do that separately, since it seems to have a slightly firmer adherence to the bone. This part will be filleted out later.

You have now reached a point where the legs and lower back have been freed from the skin. Cut off the paws inside of the skin flap, or simply cut through both paws and skin at the lowest point. There is no fur covering this area that is worth saving.

Now take a rag or, if you are using cotton gloves, as I usually do for these tasks, grab the hindquarters in one hand, the loose skin in the other, and pull till the skin is peeled up to the point of the upper chest and foreleg area.

Again make incisions on the underside of the forelegs and work the skin around them and toward the back. As before, cut off the paws and again peel and pull, this time going up to the head area as far as you can.

Upon reaching the head you will need the assistance of your knife, since the skin at the skull is again knitted very strongly to the bone. To do the animal correctly, you will actually have to skin-out over the ears, eyes, and down the tip of its nose. Don't miss those whiskers. They make fine nymph legs, feelers, and tails, not to mention whiskers for a deer-hair mouse.

Before you can free the head entirely, you will have to extend the cavity cut up through the neck to the lower jaw.

Now the real work begins. Though fleshing an animal is not difficult, it will give your muscles a good workout. The skin must be freed of all flesh and fat, and in the case of the groundhog, there is more of this than on most other species. A fairly sharp, but not too sharp, knife with a slight curve at its point end is desirable for this procedure.

Do not try to scrape the whole skin with your knife, but take small sections at a time. Try getting the knife blade just under the layer of flesh and fat with short strokes, getting it to flap out. Now take a rag for better gripping power, and grasp the fold and pull it off the skin. Sometimes you will get a fair section off the skin in one pull, and at other times only a small strip. Either way, whatever does come off, it saves that much more scraping with the knife. Work the entire skin this way by sections until you've gotten all the flesh and fat off that you can. Take a five-minute breather and again press the knife, at a slant, against the skin and scrape. By this time you'll have gotten your second wind and your arm will be stronger.

You'll notice that if you apply some pressure you will still be able to squeeze out some fluid fat from the skin. When this fluid piles up on your knife, keep wiping the blade on a rag or newspaper and continue scraping till you cannot get any more fat from the skin. If you make it to this point you'll have a nice, clean woodchuck skin, which now only requires tacking up onto a board with some small nails. This is done to prevent the skin from shrinking, and thus curling.

Drive the nails in at the head and end portions first and then stretch out each side and secure them. Do not be afraid to use enough nails.

Once tacked, I prefer to use salt on the skin of this animal because of its fatty content. It will dry in about four or five days in a dry room, after which the nails can be removed, the salt scraped off, and the clean woodchuck hide either cut into strips or packed away in its entirety.

The most important parts of the groundhog are the back, with its distinctly marked guard hairs, and the tail. Later, I'll tell you some patterns I use them for.

Road-killed woodchuck

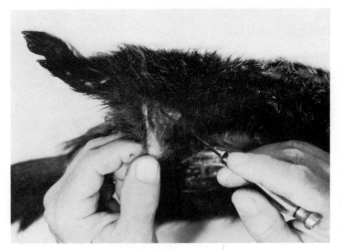

Making incision on inner hind leg

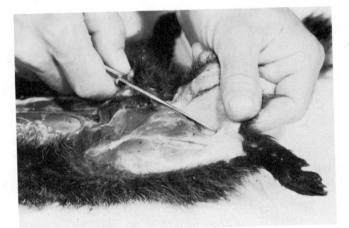

Extending incision and freeing skin from thigh

Cutting skin from leg

Pulling skin from back of 'chuck

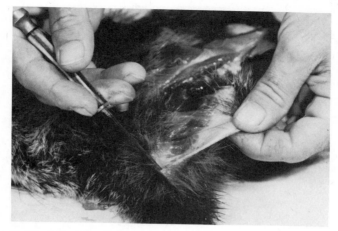

Making cut up foreleg

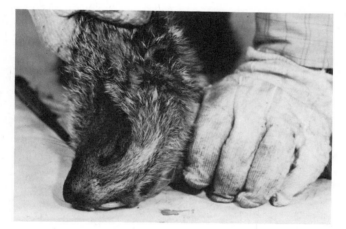

Pulling hide to head of 'chuck

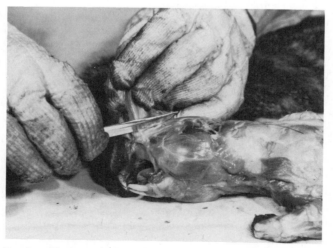

Freeing skin from head

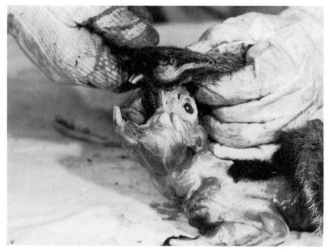

Chuck ready for final cut from head

Scraping flesh and fat from hide

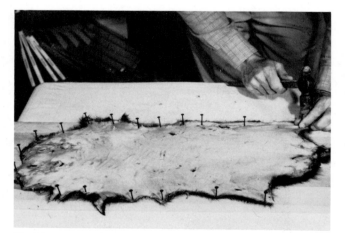

Tacking woodchuck skin to board

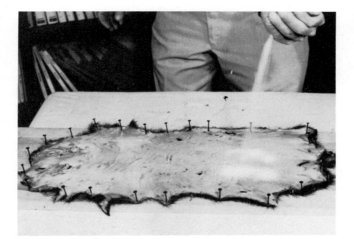

Salting down 'chuck

I skin each animal I obtain in the same manner, whether it is a squirrel or a white-tailed deer. The latter cannot, of course, be laid upon your workbench. For large animals, such as deer or antelope, it is best to hang one from the limb of a tree or railing high enough to suspend it so that the head just clears the ground. You then proceed with the same operation, starting with the hind legs and working down along the whole carcass.

I have never had the occasion to skin a moose or elk and these very large animals will present a problem because of their size. Their skin is also very tough and thick. Try cutting through a piece of dried moosehide and you will know what I mean. Your best bet on these giants is to work on sections that have been quartered, if you obtain them.

All of our animals are skinned in the "open" state, as opposed to the "cased" method used by trappers. If you know of a trapper in your locale, you can learn quite a bit from him in the matter of skinning, cleaning, and preparing hides. They will "case" most of the animals they trap, which means that the fur is literally peeled from the carcass and turned inside out, as if you were pulling off your sock without bothering to turn the outside back into place again. The peeled skin is then inserted into a wooden or expanding-metal stretcher apparatus that is made to fit the skin very snugly, again preventing shrinkage, and allowed to dry. When fully dry, the insert is removed, and you have an inside-out "cased" skin.

For our purpose the "open" method is best, since we are not interested in selling the fur to a furrier, but in using the skin for fly-tying purposes. When tacked "open," all areas are exposed on the fur side, and it can be divided into desirable sections for various purposes.

Certain animals have peculiarities that will affect the care taken during the skinning operation. Two of them are the porcupine and the rabbit.

Porcupines are not tough to skin—unless you try to skin one without knowing where to grab the animal first. You can always take hold of any of his legs at the lower portion. There are no quills there. Nor are there any on the underside of this stickler. The last place you want to take hold of him is at the tail. That part is really loaded with some of the sharpest and hardest quills.

An old wives' tale has it that a porcupine will throw his quills at you or an animal if you get close enough. This is nonsense. However, they do come off the skin easily and remain in your hand should you grab one.

When you are skinning this varmint, make sure that none of your dogs or cats, or the neighbors' pets, are around. The quills can easily lodge in a paw or snout should the friendly investigator step on some that have fallen while you are skinning. After you have finished, sweep the area clean of all fallen quills and wrap them securely before disposing of them in the garbage. The refuse collector may have a few choice words for you should he come in contact with your leftovers. He, like you, will be wearing gloves as a protection, but the quills can penetrate this fabric.

The easiest way to handle a porcupine is to lay him on his back, work the *inside* hind leg, and get the skin peeling in such a manner that the quills are always on the inside of the skin. Any pulling you do to peel the skin should be done with a dry rag, always grasping the raw skin portion. Once you've mastered your first porcupine, you'll do the next one faster than some of the other animals. When finished, I again advise salt.

Rabbits have an almost paper-thin hide, which, while easy to peel, offers the problem of easy tearing. This is one of the more common animals, both wild and domestic, you will find and be able to procure. Both are excellent—the wild variety for its natural blue gray underfur, and the domestic white, which can be dyed any color. After skinning a rabbit, it is not necessary to apply any salt. A small amount of borax will do nicely, if spread thinly and evenly over the skin. Even this is not absolutely necessary.

Generally speaking, the larger the animal, the more scraping is needed and the more salt added, simply because these animals have more natural oils and fats under the skin proper. The reverse is true with the smaller mammals.

Some of the more desirable mammals to procure would be those that live in or near the water, such as muskrat, beaver, nutria, and the weasel group, not to mention seals and other amphibious mammals that spend their lives in that environment. These animals have great luster and sheen to their coats and so make for a more lifelike imitation in patterns utilizing their fur for dubbing, or their hair for tailing and wings.

A fine example would be the polar bear, the hair of which has an almost fluorescent translucency. This animal, and rightly so, will soon be off the available list because of hunting and commercial pressure that have just about put him on the endangered species list. When an animal or bird reaches that stage I am inclined to do without, rather than see him diminish from this already ravished earth of ours.

When cutting the hides of animals, or birds for that matter, into sections for packaging and storage, *always cut the pelt from the underside.* By doing this, you will avoid damaging or cutting the guard hairs and fur. Not only will it be a neater and cleaner operation, but you will have no wasted material. Also try to avoid the use of scissors for cutting such furs. They are too indiscriminate. When cutting a piece of hide, such as a deerskin, push the point of the knife blade through the skin from underneath, fold the hide along the line to be cut, and begin. You will notice that the hairs on either side of the blade will part neatly and get out of the way as you make a path through the hair.

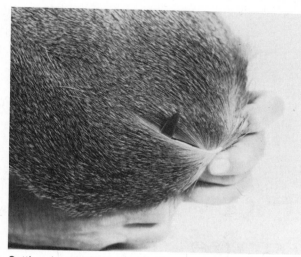

Cutting deerskin from underside

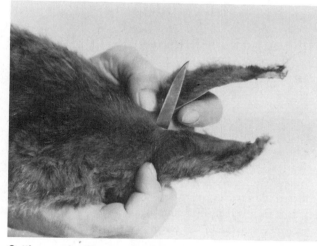

Cutting muskrat from underside

7 Preservation and Storage

Preservation of fly-tying materials is not only relegated to the items you procure on your own, but also those which you have purchased from a materials house. Your own "hoard," though you may think it large, in no way compares to the quantity a feather house must carry. In this respect you have an advantage. Though all the mail-order establishments do their utmost to supply you with the cleanest, most vermin-free, and highest-quality goods they can sell you, they are constantly receiving large shipments of merchandise, which may or may not be infected. Measures are taken to isolate these goods, and to rid them of any parasites; but in a warehouse of any size, there is bound to be an occasional accident or lapse on the part of an employee that allows a pair of "bugs" to go courting. That's all it takes.

Your supplier may send you a neck, or skin, which, when it leaves his premises, will be in what appears to be perfect condition. En route to you, larvae of moths or beetles can develop, and you will have received an infected piece of merchandise. By all means return it, if such is the case. No supplier wants you to take damaged merchandise. It is bad for business. He will, in most cases, be happy that you have returned it, so that he is made aware of the situation and can remedy it, besides replacing your purchase. If you don't report it, he will never know, and you have both lost.

Any merchandise you receive from a supply house, whether feather or fur, should be checked carefully and, if possible, isolated for a period of time, preferably in a glass container or poly bag, through which it can be observed. In the warmth of your tying area, there is enough heat to hasten the hatching of eggs, should there be any. If, however, you do not have the time to spare, there are other precautions you can take.

In the case of neck or saddle capes, or other bird plumage with the feathers on the skin, all you have to do, should you suspect infestation, is to wash them in a mild detergent. Let them soak for a half hour or so before you rinse them off with clear water. They are then best dried by the "newspaper method" described earlier, fluffed up occasionally, and when almost dry, pressed between a quantity of either old newspaper or magazines to regain their original form. Again, any misshapen feathers can be steamed back to normal shape.

Deer or calf tails, or any of the raw hides, are another matter. The skin here is much thicker and plain washing may or may not produce the desired results. In the coarser tails and furs, you will do no damage if you simply immerse them in a pot of boiling water for a few minutes. After the bath these can also be damp-dried, by wrapping in newspaper to absorb most of the moisture, and then spread out to dry in an airy room. Make certain, however, that the skin has hardened before storage. A soft skin on these hides will indicate the presence of moisture, and this will encourage mildew if you place the item in a sealed container for protection.

There are on the market many types of disinfectants and poisons, which, if sprayed on feather or fur material, would instantly kill any larvae or mature vermin. Except for paradichlorobenzene nuggets or moth crystals, I do not recommend them. Many tiers have the habit of either moistening some materials directly with their tongue, or use the hand-to-tongue procedure, to dampen a piece of hackle or hair, to make it behave properly during a tying process. Should you use a strong poison or disinfectant, the contact can be dangerous. It is wiser to use the longer, but safer course.

After your materials have either passed your isolation test or you have cleaned them yourself and are satisfied they are indeed free from pests, the surest way to keep them in that state is not necessarily the addition of deterrents, though that helps, but the protection of them in a manner that will prevent any infestation from occurring in the first place. This is a matter of storage. Since your supply will be extremely variable, both in size and kind, it becomes a multiple problem. It would be ideally efficient if all materials could be stored and cabineted in the same size container and indexed for readily accessible use. But the jar sealing your bucktails is scarcely what you need to store a few golden pheasant crests.

Jars with screw-on lids are wonderful inventions. They come in various sizes, and in most instances were made for a flytier's needs. Collect them, in all sizes you can obtain—especially the larger variety, which are becoming more difficult to come by. You can see into a glass container, and if somewhere you have erred in your earlier preparations, you will be able to view your mistake and keep it isolated in its particular jar till it is rectified.

For some of the neck capes and similar items, plastic poly bags may be used. They should be large enough so that the ends can be folded and secured with a couple of paper clips. The idea now is to prevent anything from entering, not making an exit. Cellophane bags would serve the same purpose, but they have the disadvantage of clinging too closely together and so forming a set in some of the feather and fur materials enclosed.

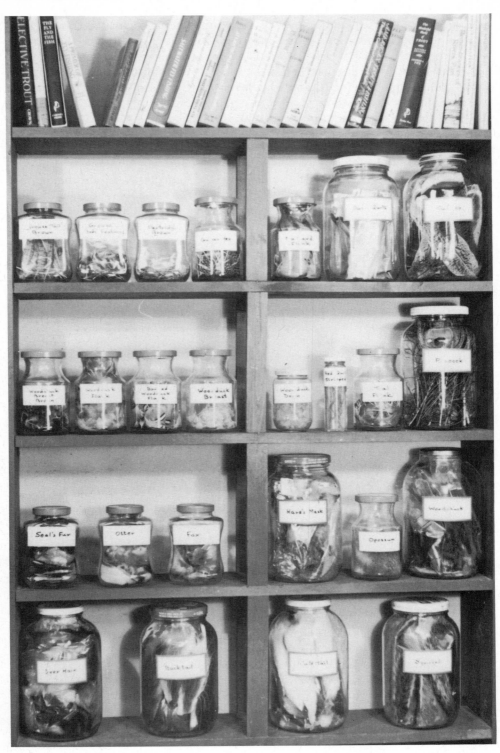

Using jars for storage

Natural Necks

1 Cream Ginger
2 Cock-y Bondhu
3 Grizzly (barred Plymouth Rock)
4 Brown
5 Dark Ginger
6 Badger
7 Red Game Variant

Dun Necks—
Natural and Dyed

8   Blue Dun (natural)
9   Bronze Dun (natural)
10 Iron Dun (natural)
11 Blue Dun (dyed)
12 Bronze Dun (photo dyed)
13 Dark Blue Dun (photo dyed)
14 Variant Dyed Bronze Dun

Wood duck skin

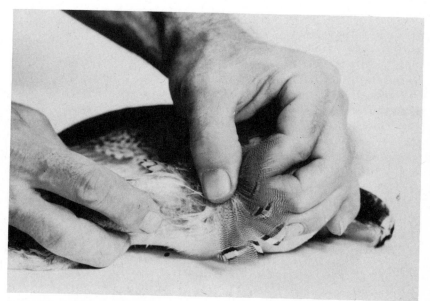

Pulling flank feathers from duck

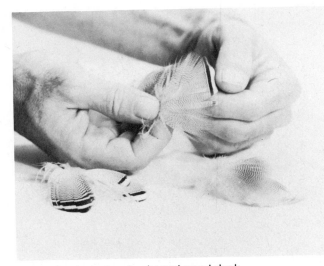

Separating barred and unbarred wood duck
flank

When using jars I sometimes add a few "para" nuggets for further protection. These are more a preventative than an outright killer, though they are advertised as capable of eliminating moths and moth larvae. The items placed in a poly bag need not be so protected, except that the larger container holding all the capes within their respective bags can have a sprinkling of these nuggets contained in them.

Be careful in the use of mothballs or paradichlorobenzene nuggets in plastic containers. There may be a chemical reaction between them, depending on the type of plastic used. Of all containers, glass is the best.

How to store is one thing, what to store is another, and finally, but most important, is the manner in which it is stored. If it flies or walks, there is useable material on the entire bird or animal. I will give you an example or two, in order that you may evolve some of your own ideas.

Let's start with the wood duck. Since we need some of its feathers, there is no point in storing the entire skin, so we will just take it apart and store its feathers separately, according to their color and use. Most of us are interested in the lemon brown flank feathers on the bird. Pluck them out. Though it would be easy enough to throw them in a jar as they are and forget them, it will be wiser if we first remove all the down from the base of each feather. Once all the fluff has been removed, they can be stored. You will find they take up much less space in the jar since they have been defluffed.

The fluff, or down, is then put into another jar. Why? Because it makes excellent dubbing. You won't have to save too much down, since it is quite plentiful. But try to save various shades of it from different birds.

The flank feathers themselves fall into two divisions: those having black and white barred tips, and those without. They are stored separately.

Stripping down flank feathers

Next, the breast, with its flared white, fan-wing-type feathers. These are also plucked, and the fluff stripped off. Incidentally, the fluffy base of any feather makes one of the favorite hiding places for moth larvae. Another good reason for using this procedure! All the white breast feathers are jarred separately from the brown ones on the upper breast, and further separation is carried through as the colors change in the neck area right up to the head.

Storing breast feathers

Though not used as extensively as those of the mallard, wings can make fine winging. If you wish your flies to have exceptionally proportioned wings, the ideal way to make them would be to use a right- and a left-wing quill coming from the same bird, from the same position. Take a pair of wings coming from one duck, whether wood duck, mallard, teal, or what have you, and first pluck the outer pointer quill from each wing. Keep these as a matching pair. Now take the second, or next quill in line from each wing and pair them up. Next the third and so on until you have all the primary wing quills off the duck, and they are evenly matched from their relative locations on each side. Keep these pairings as they are. You can place them in a narrow poly bag in pairs before jarring them. The third or fourth quill in from the pointer quills will make the best winging material, for instance, for a Black Gnat or a Blue Quill.

Cutting and pairing mallard wing quills

Matched wing quills

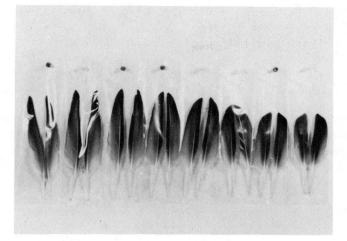

Paired quills taken from one mallard duck

Before these quills are jarred, however, you can go one step further. On each feather, whether from a duck, goose, or turkey, you can remove a quill strip from the center stem, which can be used for the ribbing of nymph patterns. To free the quill strip from the feather, immerse the entire section in a jar of water for a day or so. Some feathers require a longer immersion period than others, and some less. After it has soaked the proper amount of time, take a single-edged razor blade and make a nick in the upper, or tip, part on the stem of the quill. You will loosen the hard, outer, celluloidlike fiber from the stem proper and be able to peel the entire strip from the stem, while leaving the rest of the duck quill intact.

The strippings from various birds come in different shades, and some of them have a darker edge to the quill, answering the need for segmentation where it is required.

These stripped quills are also jarred or poly-bagged and labeled separately.

Your work is still not finished. Besides the primary quills, there are the secondaries, such as the white-tipped McGinty feather on the mallard. The same procedure applies. What about the small feathers on the upper shoulder of the wing? These range in shade from light to dark brown and from gray to black. Break them down in nomenclature, depending on the species of duck, and again store individually.

On the mallard you still have the large brown Nashua feathers to pluck and store. This is one of the more sought-after feathers for wing cases on nymphs. And it would be a crime to forget the half dozen or so bronze feathers coming off the back of the bird near the upper wing joint and slightly under it.

Also on the mallard, besides the usual barred black and white flank feather, there are some that have a darker and more distinct marking; these are used for the March Brown. This particular shade of mallard flank is also a little stiffer in texture than its lighter-shaded neighbor. Also store apart from the others.

The foregoing will give you some idea of what can be done with individual birds.

For my own tying needs, I utilize three types of storage—for immediate use, accessibility, and future use.

I have first, on my tying table, one large cedar-lined cigar box, wherein I keep a handful of necks that I know I will use for most of my tying. There are a brown, ginger, cream, grizzly, and a dun, with perhaps one or two others.

On the same table I also have another cigar box, which happens to be compartmented; it has four drawers, each of which is one and one quarter inches high, five inches deep, and nine inches long. In one of the drawers I keep very small (approximately the size of your thumb) pieces of dubbing fur of various shades. In another there are some pieces of tailing of the most used variety, also in small sections. A third holds a scattering of most needed plumage, such as a few lemon wood duck feathers, or some quills for bodies. The bottom drawer I use for some of my smaller tools and accessories.

Sitting on top of the compartmented box I have another cigar carton, of the common variety, in which I keep some of the more widely used tinsels, flosses, and wools, and on top of this I have a creation made of Styrofoam, which I glued together with some liquid cement.

This creation looks like "steps," an inch high and an inch deep. The entire structure is about a foot long and light as a feather, for which it is used. You will most likely find a pair of white and gray duck pointers imbedded in the yielding foam material, not to mention some brown turkey quills, a pair of shortened peacock sticks, both natural and stripped, and other material that will pierce the Styrofoam.

It is also an ideal contraption for implanting, or throwing as you would a dart, my dubbing needle and some other like instruments.

Depending on how much I've been working, and with what patterns, it is also usually adorned with some finished or semifinished flies, mostly of the streamer type, though there are some wets and nymphs now and again. It is not made for dry flies, since setting the hook into the foam would bend the hackle.

Though this is really my tying area, it also serves as a mini-storage space and saves steps in going to the main storage area.

The second is the main type of storage, with all its jars and complete labeling as to the contents. This will be the primary source of supply I will work from, and save in, for all the patterns I intend to tie.

The third and last type of storage is intended for the surplus material, and is out of the way, well protected for some future year when I may possibly have depleted the central storage area; if the occasion warrants, some of these materials can be traded for others.

Procure, prepare, protect, preserve, and store properly—these are the foundations for one of the most elusive and complex problems facing the average tier today. System and attention to detail are the key considerations.

⑧ Rooster Necks · Quality and Color

One of the most controversial subjects among flytiers concerns the color of various shades of rooster necks. Most people see color as it appears to them, in their own mind's eye; it is almost impossible to standardize.

Quality, on the other hand, can be learned through experience. When I speak of quality I am referring to a cape that is best suited for the purpose for which it is intended. For example, you can have a number-one quality neck with which to tie wet flies, though it will not rate as a quality neck if you are tying dries, and vice versa. Or, perhaps you are tying a large, dry salmon fly; the neck used for this fly would not be considered a quality neck if its use was intended for a 22 midge.

Quality and color are the two most important considerations a flytier should look for when purchasing a rooster neck—and in that order.

QUALITY

What should the ideal number-one, or triple grade "A," neck consist of? Since you may rarely find such a neck, *purchase one, regardless of color, when you come across a cape of this quality.*

The neck should come from a mature bird that has been killed in prime time and condition, whether it is a large barred Rock, or a buff Bantam. Necks will vary in size, but the cream of the crop are those roosters that are the largest for their species, having the stiffest, glossiest, and most resilient hackle, the barbules of which are capable of tying patterns for hook sizes from 10 to 22. In addition they should also be capable of tailing all patterns of these sizes.

This is asking quite a bit from one cape. Most number-one necks that have smaller hackles will not have the tailing for larger flies, nor will the larger-hackled capes have fibers that will tie a midge. Some tiers are of the opinion that if a cape cannot tie 24 or 28 size midges the neck is not a number one. The Canadian and Western fishermen are of the opposite opinion, and rightly so, since their patterns call for hackles from sizes 12 to 6.

Most of us are caught in the dilemma of needing both large and small hackles and, as I stated, they are a rarity to find all on one bird. So, in your collecting, do not purchase only the smaller Indian or Chinese necks of the highest quality possible, but take a second glance at some of the domestics, or the fighting cock strain, which have the quality and also the size needed for certain patterns. Soon you will be able to pair some of these capes, if they have identical shadings, and go the whole route with the matched set.

Upon picking up a neck you should first check and see if it has the size hackle you are in need of. If the particular cape can withstand the pressure, you simply hold it in one hand and bend it slightly backward so that the hackle feathers protrude from the skin. Be careful with barred Rocks and some of the thicker-skinned varieties; they are likely to crack or break off near the nape of the neck if the skin is brittle and hard. You'll then have purchased a neck whether you want it or not. This is also true of dyed capes, especially black, since the skin on these has shrunk from the heat of the dyebath and again becomes brittle because of loss of natural oils from the skin.

All of these necks can be softened, if you take a little time with them, by the application of some glycerine to the skin side. On a dyed neck this may be accomplished more easily if the cape is first immersed in warm water, allowing the tissue to soften before applying the glycerine. Work it just a little and let it set, and you'll soon find that you will be able to bend the particular cape without snapping off the tip.

While you have the hackles protruding from the neck, and have isolated one to check the barbule size, you might also fan the feathers with your free finger and see how fast they move back to position. This will determine their resiliency or "bounce." The faster they bounce, the more alive the hackle usually is, and the greater the stiffness. A soft-hackled neck will not bounce back very fast, which often indicates excessive web in the feather or a poor grade of neck. A webby neck is not necessarily a second-rater; many of them will make fine hackles for wet flies.

While you still have the hackles protruding, hold them up to any available light. Sunlight would be best. Notice the sheen or sparkle. Does it look alive? Turn the neck around and look at the back side of the feathers. They will not be the same shade as the outer side, but they should be close. If you look on the underside of a hackle feather from a black neck, you will notice that the color here is more an iron dun than a true black; the latter is hard to find in both true color and quality.

As long as you still have the feathers extended from the cape, you might also poke a finger between the hackles and search for any pinfeathers. These are short feathers just beginning to emerge. If there are too many, the bird has not yet fully matured or become prime for that season, since all his winter plumage has not grown out. There are more feathers on a prime bird. Some have such a heavily feathered coat that it actually swells outward from the neck.

You can release the hackles now and let them collapse back onto the skin. The kind of neck you are poring over will determine what you will look for next, at the very tip. For instance, in the case of a badger, with its black center and white or cream outer hackle, you want to make sure that this stripe is predominant in all the hackles, even to the smallest. Here you will have to use some judgment; for instance, you may not use the hackles at the very tip if you are tying the

Absolutely essential, of course, is a stove or heating apparatus, whether electric or gas, with two or more burners. Gas is better since the heat is more controllable.

One optional gadget you may wish to use if you have never dyed anything before is a meat thermometer; this can be inserted into the water to obtain the temperature of the dyebath. Temperature affects the results of the operation, but only in the depth of the shade desired. Temperatures pertaining to specific materials will be discussed as we get to them.

Now to begin. Take one of the dyeing pans and fill it one-third full of water. The average size of this container for home dyeing will hold from one to two gallons of water, when full.

For my own dyeing I use two sizes, besides an additional pan in each size for light and dark shades. I use the smaller pan for dyeing up a few necks or other small-sized material, and the larger for such cumbersome items as deer tails, calf tails, and body hair.

For this first attempt let's assume you are attempting to dye a half-dozen rooster necks a blue dun. Fill one pan a third full with water and place it on your stove to heat. Bring the water to a boil and then add your dye, in this case either a Rit Gray or a Veniard Blue Dun. Amounts needed will be covered later. Adding the dye to the water while it is boiling will cause it to dissolve more rapidly.

After you have added the dye, pour a few drops of an agent, or "fixer," such as acetic acid or, if you do not have that, plain vinegar. If you use the latter, you will have to use a bit more, since the acetic acid in vinegar has been diluted. It will be less expensive if you buy it in pure form from a pharmaceutical house or chemical supply corporation. Ask for Glacial Acetic Acid. It is a liquid.

The reason for the addition of acid or any fixing agent is to allow the dye to burn into the fibers and penetrate, making the color "fast." If you do not use it, you may find after washing that the shade you were seeking has also been rinsed away.

When you have added both the dye and the acetic acid, take a spoon and stir, making sure all the dye has been dissolved. Now turn off the flame.

Using a pair of pot holders, take the pan and put it under cold running water in the sink; cool the solution to about 160°. You should be able to place your finger in it without scalding. Experience as to how much water to add will come with time, and that is why, though I no longer use one myself, I recommend a thermometer. In any event, the added water should make your pan a little more than half full. The bath is now ready for your material.

With your tongs, grasp the presoaked and cleaned rooster necks, one at a time, and as you immerse them, swish them back and forth in the dyebath to ensure penetration of the dye all the way to the base of the feathers. Do not play with the one neck too long, but go on to the next neck in turn, and then the next again, until they are all immersed in the bath. Even so, you will find that the last to enter the bath will be of a lighter blue dun shade than the first.

When all the necks are swimming around together, keep them in motion with the aid of your tongs in order to obtain the utmost uniformity. If they are allowed to lie still, you will find that the parts of the neck most exposed to the bath water will be of a darker hue than those hackles which lie under some of the upper ones. The swishing motion ensures even coloration throughout.

If you have used the correct amount of dye and water, you will obtain the correct shade you are searching for, and the water in the dyebath will become almost clear—rusty, but clear enough to see through.

Upon completion in the bath, the contents of the entire pan or container may be spilled into the sink. At this point you may as well take a sponge and clean the pan for future use. A little soap on the sponge will turn the trick, along with a little elbow grease.

The dyed necks are then picked up, one by one, and rinsed under the faucet to wash away any excess dye left on from their bath. After you have rinsed one, lay it on its back, feather side up. Lay the next one on top of it with the feather side down. Whether wet or dry, capes and also furs should always be placed skin to skin, or feather to feather when piling them in bundles, in order to keep any grease on the skin side from adhering to the feather or fur side of another.

In this order pile up your six necks. When they are all in a heap, take them as a unit and squeeze the water from them, getting them as dry as your hands can squeeze.

Now lay them on newspaper to dry, and go into the fluffing and drying procedure mentioned in the previous chapter. That's all there is to it, except that types of materials and varying shades all have their peculiarities.

YELLOW. This is the easiest of all colors to dye, and nearly all companies have a good grade of dye in this shade. My own preference for this color, and its lighter and darker relations, is Herter's Drake Yellow and Deep Yellow, as well as those sold by Hille and Veniard's.

With a yellow dye, you will need little, if any, of the acid for fixing. It takes very well. It also requires very little swishing. Most materials, if kept immersed, will soon take on the full yellow shade. When dyeing rooster necks, saddles, or similar feathers yellow, you can use a low degree of temperature. They will, in fact, take the dye when cold.

Other items—such as deer tail, calf tail, and deer body hair—require a slightly different approach. When dyeing these yellow, or any other shade, it is best to fill your container about two-thirds full of water; leave your water on the burner even after it has reached the boiling point. Though the dye will perform on the hair, only the outer extremities of the hairs will receive the full effect. Unless the tail is actually boiled in the bath, the hair near the stem will be lighter in shade. Boiling water will also cause flow and agitation desirable for uniformity. The material in the bath will not be harmed by this procedure since these particular fibers are very tough and can take a great deal of punishment. I do not recommend this, however, for necks and softer materials.

On the other hand, polar bear hair has to be dyed in a cool or lukewarm dyebath. If you put it into water just a little too hot, the hairs, as they touch the sides and bottom of the pan, will singe and lose their tapered effect. Polar bear hair requires cool temperature and a long—perhaps a day or so—immersion period in order for the dye to penetrate properly.

Dyeing necks and similar feathers yellow takes but a few minutes.

Boiling deer tails yellow takes approximately a half hour to get a complete effect. Don't keep the flame up high, but turn it so that the solution simmers.

When you remove deer or calf tails, care should be taken that they are gently but firmly squeezed to rid them of the excess water. Do not wring them. Wringing will now tear the softened skin. These tails should then be wrapped in newspaper, which will absorb any excess moisture, leaving the tails or body hair damp.

They are next laid out neatly on fresh dry newspaper, with the skin side to the print. As they dry they are also fluffed and changed around so that air can move freely through all parts until the skin has hardened, indicating absence of moisture; this is necessary if they are to be stored.

ORANGE. Here again, there is not too much difficulty in obtaining a good dye. Any of the aforementioned companies carry it.

Other than plain orange, a color resembling the fruit of the same name is called "Hot" Orange, and this is very bright indeed. It is sold in a straight dye and so listed by Veniard's, though it can be obtained by adding a small amount of red to the regular orange dye. "Hot" Orange is used in many saltwater and salmon patterns.

RED. The best results I have had with this color were using a combination of two of the dyes sold by Herter's. I mix about half and half of their Scarlet Red and Crimson Red dyes and obtain a bright fiery shade.

On this particular dye, however, it does not pay to skimp. You'll need more dye powder than for the yellows or oranges. Materials should also be left in the dyebath longer than average to reach the desired result.

The only trouble with red, as a color, is the problem of making it "fast." Did you ever own a red sweater and notice that when your wife or mother washes it, she does it separately from other garments? This is due to the fact that red is seldom "fast"; it always seems to run, or wash away some of its pigment with each rinsing, no matter how old or how long it has been used.

GREEN. This is a fairly easy shade to obtain in all of the variations from light to dark. Specific colors, such as Supervisor Green, or Insect Green, are sold as such by the supply houses that carry dyes.

You can obtain your own depth of green by starting with the lightest dye of that shade, and then adding darker shades as you progress, until you arrive at the desired result.

If you wish to make your own Insect Green dye—a green with a hint of yellow in it—you will have to start by using yellow as your base, and adding a light green to achieve the effect. This basic rule applies for all color mixing: *Always use the lighter dye and add the darker in small quantity until you reach the exact shade you want.*

PINK. This is also a very easy color to dye. You can scarcely make a mistake with it, even if you add too much. For this shade I use the ordinary commercial brand called Rit in the pink shade.

BLUE. Again, no problem, whether light, medium, or dark. All the supply houses will list a "Silver Doctor" blue, and also such others as kingfisher blue, bluebottle blue, teal blue, and so forth. Your local department store will also carry various shades of this basic color.

For Silver Doctor blue you will want a light, but not pale, blue dye.

BLACK. A very important shade, but as far as I'm concerned, it is one of the toughest and messiest to obtain in true depth. Home dyeing of black always seems to leave a vague hint of brown or blue no matter how long the material is immersed.

In boiling to black, you simply leave the deer tail or calf tail in the bath until it is all black. Necks and similar materials, however, require a temperature less than boiling, and black dye seems to take forever to penetrate into the fibers. Nevertheless, with perseverance and much redyeing, it can be accomplished.

There is a fringe benefit in trying to dye brown rooster necks black and not succeeding. One day, after having a number of necks soak in a black dyebath for a few hours, I assured myself they really looked black; but when I removed, rinsed, and thoroughly dried the necks, I obtained a beautiful dark brown and glossy Coachman color.

WOOD DUCK. The simplest dye I have found for obtaining this shade is that sold by Veniard's. It requires no mixing. The name of their dye for this purpose is Summer Duck, and it imitates the coloration of a natural wood duck flank feather as closely as possible.

To be sure, it is also available through some of the other houses, and you can also arrive at the shade by mixing brown and yellow dye in the correct proportions. In the latter case, let me remind you to start with the yellow as your base, and add the brown as needed until the desired effect is reached.

In dyeing the mallard flank, which is the main purpose of this dye, you must allow the feathers to soak for a long time, preferably overnight, in a grease-dispelling solution. When they are ready for the dyebath, pour them into your colander and rinse them thoroughly with lukewarm water until all the soap and grime have been rinsed from the feathers.

A few of the flanks may escape through the fine holes of this utensil, but most will remain there, and when they have been completely rinsed, they are transferred to the bath.

Let them soak in the dyebath for a longer period of time than usual. Approximately four or five hours will be fine. This accomplished, they are retransferred into the colander, to be strained of excess dye.

Next, grasp and ball them up in your hands, as if you were kneading dough, and squeeze out the water. Now lay them on a large square of newspaper and wrap them up in it until the paper has absorbed the excesses your hand could not squeeze out. You can then dry them slowly by spreading them on more paper, and fluffing them now and again.

Another method of drying flank feathers, or any loose plumage, is to borrow your wife's hair dryer. Take a large bag of brown paper or poly, and attach it to the exhaust end of the dryer—the part that blows the hot air onto the head. Make sure the bag is securely fastened. After you have enclosed your damp wood duck feathers, turn on the dryer and within half an hour you'll have the driest, fluffiest wood duck flank imaginable, all ready to be packed and stored, or used.

BROWN. Light? Medium? Dark? The varying shades of this color may be obtained in several ways. The first is to try the differing dyes sold in department stores and the mail-order houses, and try with each shade, noting well in writing the results of the particular brand. I have had dyes labeled Dark Brown that came nowhere near that shade.

Don't forget to add the agent (acid) to this dye, or you will obtain very much less than the desired end. This also pertains to the greens and olives. I recall an instance where it appeared that the results of my dyebath would be the exact shade of olive I was searching for. Upon rinsing, all the necks emerged with a dirty yellow hue. All the olive green had been washed away because I had neglected to add the agent.

Rit makes a good dye for obtaining a medium shade of brown. It is called Cocoa Brown.

The second way of obtaining your shade of brown is to take a standard brown dye, and then add black in small quantities until you reach your goal. A good black to use as an additive is that sold by Herter's.

OLIVE. As I mentioned in the chapter on rooster necks, this color is confusing to many tiers. Green olive, medium olive, dark olive, brown olive, olive dun, and others are among the various listings of this shade.

If the dyes listed under these particular names do not give you the color you want, revert to mixing your own, using the lightest of the olives as your base and adding the darker or off-shades until you achieve the proper results.

All these formulas, once you have obtained them, should be written down in order to save time at some future date.

BLUE DUN, BRONZE DUN. This is the color most dyed by the flytier, and it is primarily used on rooster necks.

Many of the so-called "Breed" necks, the half-fast badgers and chinchillas, and some of the lighter variants are excellent necks to dye to this color. Why? Because they appear closer to a natural blue dun than if dyed from a pure white or cream neck.

Many tiers believe a blue dun should be a gray neck with a blue cast—the shade, as a whole, being of uniform coloration. This is about as far away as you can go from a natural blue dun shade, even though you are using a dye manufactured for that purpose.

Most professional tiers will select necks that have a broken pattern, and some will even use pure chinchilla or a top-grade barred Rock to dye blue dun, just to obtain the "breakup" effect.

Dark creams and light variants will make excellent bronze and rusty duns respectively. Here is an opportunity to utilize some of those necks that never seem to fit any pattern. Dye them. If you don't like the result, you can always go to the extreme and dye them again, all the way to black, which surely has a use.

Most of the dyes sold as blue or bronze dun by the mail-order houses are quite good and will do the job just as they are. If, however, you wish a particular shade, you can change the color by the addition of some brown dye—or, for darkness, some black. Use these additions sparingly, because if you go over the brink, you will not be able to come back to the shade you had in mind. Not for that dye-bath, at least.

Many tiers complain that when dyeing rooster necks or other materials having feather or fur on the skin, the skin becomes hard and brittle. If you wish your skin to remain soft, you can, just before the neck is completely dry, rub a little glycerine to its skin side and let it soak in. Work it a few times for a few successive days, and you'll have a soft-skinned, yet dyed, cape.

How much dye should you use for a particular dyebath? This variable is affected by the color of the dye itself, the strength of the specific manufactured dye, the temperature of the water and its volume, and the nature of the material. Yet it can all be summed up with one basic rule: *Use as small a quantity of any given dye as possible and work toward the shade desired by adding more as it is needed.*

You can always add, but you can never take away, or lighten a shade once it has been established. Thus, if you are dyeing a blue dun rooster neck, start with a quarter teaspoonful or less of dye. If you are obtaining a light blue dun and want a medium shade, take the neck out of the bath, add a bit more dye, reboil, cool, and again immerse the neck in the bath. You will find that the shade has darkened.

There is one other important point to keep in mind: *Any color when wet will appear darker than when it has fully dried.* This suggests there is some guesswork involved in obtaining the *exact* shade desired, and to a degree there is. It may occur to you after the necks have been dried that they are indeed lighter than you thought they would be. However, you have now learned to what degree they are lighter, and the next time you do the same dyeing operation you will know that to obtain the desired shade of blue dun, you will have to add just a bit more dye, so that the neck in the bath will really appear darker than you want it, but upon drying will approximate the image of the color you had in mind.

To assist you further, all supply houses and department stores that sell dyes include with their product full instructions on the use of their particular dyes.

SPECIAL DYEING FOR DUNS

I cannot recall ever having seen mention of the following process used in the dyeing of rooster necks to the shades of bronze and blue dun. It is the most excellent, though slightly more expensive, method you can use in this procedure. It is called *photo dyeing*.

For this process I am indebted to my good friend, and the photographer of the pictures in this book, Gus Nevros, of Manhasset, New York. Gus does his own developing, as a true photographer should, and is familiar with the various chemicals used in the process. For that reason I asked him one day to do a little experimenting for me, using some of his equipment. The results were far beyond my expectations.

One of the major reasons for utilizing this process of photo dyeing is that it is done in a cold bath. You do not have to preheat water or immerse necks in a hot solution to arrive at desired dun shades. Consequently, when the neck has been processed, its skin has not shriveled as it would while using the standard method of dyeing.

Other reasons for photo dyeing a rooster neck are that a color truer to the natural is achieved, and a natural sheen is actually added to the neck, instead of having been lost, as it is in some cases when other methods are used.

You do not have to be a photographer to accomplish what we have done. It is essentially simple, and for the most part you have only to read the instructions on the labels of the various photographic materials used for developing films and apply them for the mixture of your own solutions when dyeing.

You will need the following equipment and supplies:

(1) Three stainless steel or porcelain pans, capable of holding at least one-half gallon of water.

(2) One large screw-top jar capable of holding a gallon of water. A jar of this type may be difficult to find, but they are still available. Ask your grocer to save some for you.

(3) Two glass containers in quart size, like those used for milk or orange juice. Also with screw-on lids.

(4) Two pairs of stainless steel tongs—one to be used only for the silver nitrate solution, and the other for use in the developer, neutralizer, and fixer solutions.

(5) A pair of well-fitting, preferably thin, rubber gloves.

(6) A scale capable of measuring quantities of powdered chemicals, down to one-eighth of an ounce. This does not have to be an expensive affair since you are not doing photographic work. A few grains more or less in your solutions will not affect the outcome to any noticeable degree.

(7) Some small flat-bottomed paper cups, like those used at a water cooler. These may first be weighed in themselves and then used for the transfer of chemicals, after that quantity has been weighed, taking into consideration the original weight of the cup.

(8) A pan for soaking rooster necks. You can use the pan normally used for any of your other soaking and dyeing for this purpose.

(9) A pile of old newspapers.

The photographic supplies you will have to purchase from a photo supply company are:

(1) Silver nitrate. This will be your most expensive item. It usually goes for about $6.00 per ounce. If you intend to do quite a bit of this type of dyeing, which is likely once you have seen the results, it would be less expensive if you buy it by the pound from a chemical supply house.

Utensils for photo dyeing process

(2) Developer. There are several of these, two of the most effective being Dektol and D-76, both of which are manufactured by Kodak. Expense here is negligible. Other developers on the market will also produce results and you may wish to experiment with them.

(3) An acetic acid solution, to be used as a neutralizer. This is also sold by the manufacturer as is. However, if you wish to mix your own, the proportion for the solution is eight parts water and three parts acetic acid. This solution is then further added to water at the ratio of two ounces per gallon. It may be critical for the photographer to be exact in this formula when developing film, but for your work it is of no great consequence if the measurements vary slightly either way. I have had just as much success by pouring a tablespoon or so into a pan of water and stirring it.

(4) A fixer, sometimes called Hypo, also made by Kodak, is used in the final step in setting the shade attained. This product, also, is inexpensive.

The intensity of the shade you desire in dyeing your necks either a bronze or blue dun will depend on the strength of the silver nitrate solution.

The shade, whether blue or bronze dun, will depend on the type of developer used, in addition to the original color of the neck.

For the intensity, I use three different solutions of silver nitrate.

(1) For light shades of dun—pale to light blue or bronze. Measure one-eighth ounce of silver nitrate into two quarts of water.

(2) For medium shades. Measure one-quarter to three-eighths ounce of silver nitrate to two quarts of water.

(3) For dark shades. Measure five-eighths to three-quarters ounce of silver nitrate to two quarts of water.

The above ratios are the correct mixtures when using the one gallon jar the rooster necks are soaked in. A container this size will comfortably hold six necks at one time and allow the silver nitrate to penetrate the fibers easily.

After a certain period of time the silver nitrate solution will weaken and lose its effectiveness. I would advise you to save and store all the necks you are going to dye and do them all at one sitting in order to obtain the most from this chemical. I have been able to dye up to forty necks in one afternoon using this procedure. At other times, when I had left the solution standing for a week or two and went back to do some more necks, I noticed substantial loss of power in the silver nitrate, resulting in lighter-colored shades of dun.

As you progress in the photo-dyeing process you can vary the strengths of the silver nitrate to your own desires. You will be able to obtain shades ranging from a pale, watery dun to an almost black, charcoal gray shade.

The mixtures of powder to water for solutions of the developers and fixers are clearly indicated on the product. Use them just as prescribed. When you purchase them you will discover that they come in small- and large-sized boxes. Buy the ones marked for mixture with one-half U.S. gallon. This pertains mainly to the Dektol and D-76 developers. Use the entire contents for any one dyeing operation. If you use only part, and leave the remainder exposed for future use, the powder will be affected by exposure to air.

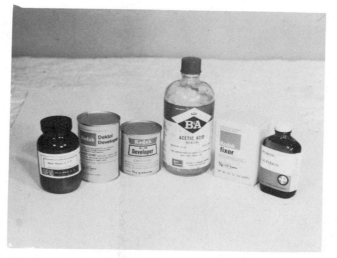

Chemicals for photo dyeing

"Developing" silver-nitrated neck

Neutralizing photo-dyed neck

Setting color on dyed neck

The following is a step-by-step process for the photo dyeing of rooster necks.

As with all dyeing, allow your necks to be well soaked in a pan of water for not less than four hours. Use a mild dishwashing detergent to rid the neck of any grease or grime. When the allotted time has elapsed, rinse and wash the necks thoroughly so they are as clean as you can get them. Place them in a pan of clear, fresh water until they are ready for use.

Place from four to six of the necks, no more, into the silver nitrate solution. This is your one gallon jar filled half full of water and having the desired amount of silver nitrate dissolved in it, depending on the depth of shade you are striving for. *Allow the necks to remain in the silver nitrate for no less than an hour.* Every now and again agitate the necks gently by moving them around with your tongs to allow the nitrate to penetrate to all parts of the neck. This will make the difference of uniformity in shade once you place the neck in the developer.

When the necks have been immersed in the silver nitrate solution for the proper time, pick one of them up with your tongs and allow the excess liquid to drip from it as much as possible, yet not waiting too long, and transfer it into the pan containing the developer solution.

If you should accidentally drop the tongs into the developer solution, rinse them off before using them again in the silver nitrate; if you don't, the developer will react with the nitrate and turn that expensive solution into a murky brown.

When you are performing the photo-dyeing operation, wear your rubber gloves or you will have stains on your hands that will not wash off easily. Also, unless you have a work area where it does not matter if a few stains accumulate, I would advise you to protect the kitchen area—where the sink usually is—with quantities of spread-out newspaper.

As soon as you have dropped the neck into the developer solution, grasp your other pair of tongs and push the neck down into it. Next, grasp the neck with your tongs and swish it back and forth gently so that the developing solution permeates all parts.

If you use Dektol as a developer, you will find that there is an instant reaction, transforming the neck almost immediately into your shade of dun. D-76 is a slow reactor, and it may take anywhere from ten minutes to an hour for the neck to turn into the desired shade. In the latter case do not think that the solution is weak. It is just the nature of this particular chemical combination.

After you have placed your first neck or two into the developer, you will find that these solutions have turned a murky brown or gray shade. They are still good for at least another ten or twelve necks, so do not let the color of the solution disturb you.

When you have achieved the uniformity and shading desired, pick up the neck with the tongs, allow the excess solution to drip off, and place the neck in the neutralizer solution, which is the acetic acid mixture. This will stop any further action between the silver nitrate and the developer. Swish the neck for a minute or two, and then transfer it into your final or "fixer" solution. This will set the color you have attained. Allow it to remain in the last pan for approximately five or ten minutes. It is possible, as you go through the process with the other necks, that you may have two or three necks lying in the fixer solution simultaneously. It will not harm them to stay in the solution over ten minutes.

After the color has been set, these finished necks are removed from the last pan, rinsed off in clear running water, squeezed to remove excess water, and placed on or between newspapers in order that further moisture may be absorbed. The fluffing, drying, and pressing procedures are now employed in the same manner as with the other necks used in the previous dyeing process.

I have found that Dektol will produce more of the bronze hues, the degrees varying with the original shade of the rooster neck itself.

For the blue duns, D-76 is my choice, whether for a pale gray or a charcoal shade.

One of the advantages of the photo-dyeing process, in addition to those already mentioned, is that necks in light shades of brown, all variants and breeds can be utilized. You will achieve from these necks an extremely natural appearing dun neck of a superlative grade.

On one occasion, I took photo dyeing a step further and used it in conjunction with the regular dyeing process mentioned earlier. My object was to attain a special color of olive—medium-dark olive green with brown overtones. I first dyed a few white and cream necks in a standard yellow dyebath, fairly cool in order not to shrink the skin, using acetic acid as the fixer. After having thoroughly rinsed the dyed yellow necks, I immersed them in the silver nitrate solution, letting them soak the required period of time. They were then processed through both the D-76 and Dektol developers, some necks in one and the remainder in the other.

I got my olive neck.

If you wish to experiment further—and this photo-dyeing process can become an intriguing affair once you have visited a photographic supply house—you can purchase some of the color toners sold in these establishments. There are a variety of these into which a presoaked neck can be immersed, set, and then placed in the silver nitrate. Since the original color determines the result, the changing of the natural to various shades and tints will lead to a further unexplored field of color variation.

When you have finished with your photo-dyeing project, place all your chemicals in a safe place, out of the reach of children. These chemicals *can be poisonous* if swallowed and caustic if handled improperly. Discretion is called for.

BLEACHING

This word has two meanings for the flytier. At times the term refers to the burning off of the flue from a peacock eye to obtain a stripped quill for the Quill Gordon pattern. In other instances, it applies to the process of submerging a piece of fur or feather in a solution of peroxide in order to obtain a lighter color. For our purposes the former method will be called "burning," the latter "bleaching."

For the "burning" process all you will need is a bottle of common household Clorox and some baking soda. For utensils, a pair of large dishes and a set of stainless steel tongs or tweezers will suffice.

Peacock eyes, condor quills, if you have any left, goose or what have you are simply immersed in a full-strength or slightly water-diluted solution of Clorox. With your tweezers, grasp and swish your material about until all the flue has dissolved from the main stem.

This operation takes but minutes, depending upon whether the solution is full strength or not, and you will have to stay and observe the material until the flue has disintegrated. Then remove the peacock or other quill from the Clorox and allow it to soak in a solution of baking soda and water. Agitate the fibers a bit to insure penetration to all parts. The baking soda will act as a neutralizer to the chemical action of the Clorox. Finally, rinse your quills off in clear water and allow them to dry. That's all there is to it.

Incidentally, many of you who tie the Red Quill pattern may be interested to know that the quills for this pattern may be obtained by using the above "burning" process. I was first made aware of this by John Goodleaf, of Wantagh, New York, a first-rate tier.

Utensils, chemicals for bleaching and burning

Soaking peacock in Clorox

Deflued peacock

Rhode Island Red neck and trimmed
feather ready for burning

Immersing beaver in peroxide for bleaching

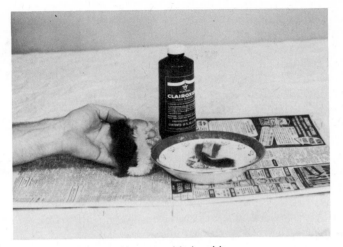

Natural and bleached beaver, side by side

His recommendation was to take a number of Rhode Island Red rooster hackles and cut away the fibers from the center stem, shearing them off as closely as possible. This leaves you with a bare stem that has a stubby flue. Having prepared a quantity, you then immerse them in Clorox solution in the same manner as a peacock eye, and the remaining hackle stubs are allowed to dissolve. After neutralization and rinsing, the fiber is perfect for the Red Quill body.

John goes a bit further, and instead of drying and storing, he places the stripped quills in an empty olive jar, which is then filled with a solution of glycerine and water. In this preservative he has been able to keep them for years, and then they of course require no presoaking before use. They will not lose their red quill color during the Clorox process.

For the Red Quill, or any other defibered hackle quill—such as that on some of the many "Breadcrust" patterns—this procedure is preferable to the stripping of the hackle quill by hand because the stripping method *removes* the inherent color of the center stem on each side where the fibers have been pulled.

The "burning" process applies almost exclusively to the defluing of such quills as we have just mentioned.

Peroxide was discovered by brunettes who wanted to have more fun, and in turn by flytiers, who tend to discover all things eventually. For the latter, its primary use is to bleach certain furs and hides to a lighter shade.

I cannot recommend peroxide for the bleaching of a brown rooster neck, of which there is always a surplus, to a more desirable shade of ginger. Bleaching a rooster neck, or any feather, destroys the substance and texture of the fibers. If you try it with a red game neck, you will find, after it has arrived at the ginger shade you're striving for, that the tip ends of the hackles have a slight curl to them, and that the hackle itself has lost its original luster; in addition, the whole feather right into the stem will have become weakened and brittle. *Don't bleach any feathers.*

It is a simple matter to place furs into a dish or pan containing a full-strength solution of hydrogen peroxide—which is usually sold in a 20 percent volume mixture—and to leave it immersed until the appropriate coloration has been achieved. The length of time the fur is immersed will depend on the kind it is and its original color. This can vary from a few hours to a few days.

I recently tried bleaching a piece of muskrat and a piece of gray Australian opossum. The opossum turned to a cream shade overnight, while it took almost two full days to attain a shade of tannish ginger with the muskrat. While the opossum was of a lighter gray, the texture of the fibers was, in addition, of a lesser density than that of the muskrat. The piece of muskrat was from the animal's back—dark, blue gray.

Bleaching is only recommended when the natural shade of a desirable piece of fur is unobtainable, or when it is used to lighten the fur's color in order to dye it to a red, green, olive, or other unnatural shade. Bleaching and then dyeing can be accomplished with a little patience and perseverance. This will involve the two separate processes. Needless to say, the dual process will not help the fur, but if intended primarily for dubbing purposes, it will be all right.

Blending furs is another method of arriving at certain shades of color without the use of bleaching and dyeing. This may be accomplished in two ways.

Shearing rabbit skin

Dry mixing rabbit and seal fur

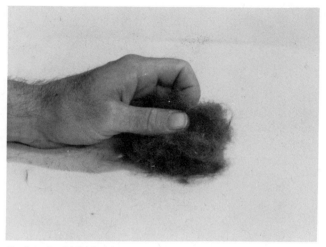

Seal and rabbit blend

(1) The dry method. Cut the fur from two shades you wish to blend and shred it with a pair of scissors. Take the cuttings into your fingers and inter-mingle them by alternately mixing and pulling them apart until the mass achieves a uniformity throughout.

Seal fur is excellent for this type of blending, either with itself or in conjunc-tion with softer furs. The latter use will also enable you to dub seal fur more readily if you have mixed.it with some of the clingier furs, such as rabbit or opossum, while still retaining the inherent luster associated with the fur of the seal.

Wet blending seal and rabbit fur

Blended seal and rabbit in jar of water

Blended mass of rabbit and seal drying on newspaper

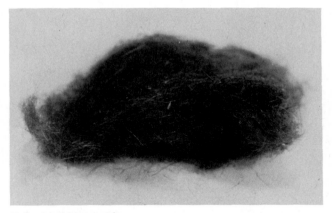

Fully dried blended fur

(2) The wet method. Blending may be accomplished by placing the clippings of the various shaded furs in a jar of water and then shaking the jar sharply. The resultant glob is then squeezed to rid it of as much excess water as possible, placed on newspaper or paper toweling, and allowed to dry.

If you wish to learn even more about the bleaching process, go to a beauty salon, or ask your wife to do it for you, since this may prove slightly less embarrassing, and ask the proprietor what formula he uses to make a brunette into a blonde or redhead. These establishments have quite a few concoctions and could recommend some that will send you farther afield in this area. However, this can become expensive. You may also wind up with more toners and conditioners than you know what to do with.

10 Uncommon Uses of Natural Materials

Collecting various materials can become an obsession in itself. A most enjoyable one, assuredly—yet in the lifetime of any addicted tier, the total sum of his warehouse will never be utilized or dented in the slightest degree. We all keep collecting and stockpiling to our dying day, because we know that we will have a use for this or that sometime in the future.

However, if we do not use or try to create with some of our newfound supplies, the edge may wear a little in our endeavor of only collecting. Therefore, it is time to tie with some of this material, hopefully giving you a fresh approach to some new patterns and improving methods of tying some of the old standards.

Since we spent quite a few moments with the common groundhog, or woodchuck, we can start with him and see how an old standby pattern, which has given a number of tiers a few frustrations, may be tied, not only more simply, but more effectively as well. I am referring to the Irresistible, which calls for a wing and tail made from deer body hair.

The body of the Irresistible is also made of deer body hair, clipped to a tapering shape. This takes a bit of extra doing but creates no serious problem—and it *does* make for a very buoyant fly. However, every time I try to get the wings and the tail to stand erect in a fairly straight grouping, I have difficulty keeping the deer body hair from flaring.

If I replace the wings and tail with the guard hairs taken from the back of a woodchuck, I not only get them to behave properly, but I have a fairly stiff fiber for these parts of the fly, in addition to an effectively marked and well defined wing and tail. Thus, try tying the Irresistible using the following:

IRRESISTIBLE

Wing: guard hairs from back of woodchuck
Tail: guard hairs from back of woodchuck
Body: natural gray deer body hair, clipped and tapered
Hackle: blue dun rooster neck hackle
Head: black

Irresistible

Incidentally, you will note that the head is black, and so tied with that color thread. However, when you tie in the deer body hair and spin it onto the shank of the hook for the body, try using either a white or light-gray thread. It will blend perfectly with the natural deer hair.

On the Irresistible or the Rat-faced McDougal, or for that matter any clipped deer-hair flies, which also have wings and hackle, the easiest procedure is first to tie in the tail, then spin the body, tie off with thread, remove the unfinished fly from the vise, and clip the deer body hair to shape. It may then be reinserted into the vise, in order to tie in the wings and hackle which will now not be obscured or hindered by the flared hairs.

One of my favorite patterns is very little known, at least in this area. It is also tied with woodchuck guard hair. When I first showed the pattern to a few friends and tiers, I asked them if they could identify the wing material. Guesses ranged from badger hair, wolf, squirrel, and a few other animals with similar hair for tailing; none mentioned woodchuck.

When I said what it was they were quite surprised. I believe one of the reasons for this unexpected reaction is that a groundhog, when viewed from a distance, as is normally the case, appears to be of an ordinary (even dirty) shade of brown. But if the guard hairs are examined closely, you will notice that they have a luster and life, not to mention perfect barring, depending on the individual 'chuck.

This fly is of the streamer variety, and has a strange name, The Llama. It was first introduced to me by a tier in Wisconsin, Ray Benedict. He said the fly was described in an old, out-of-print, English fly-tying book, and that locally it was tied by one of the native Indians. I was also informed that it was the only fly to take a limit of trout on a certain river consistently, over all other patterns. Only live bait seemed to outfish it.

The Llama

I accepted most of this information with the usual grain of salt until a close friend, Bob Sater, tied a few Llamas for himself and reported some fascinating results. Very simply, he caught some trout—which is not the usual case on Long Island's so-called trout streams. His success induced me to tie a few of this pattern for myself and some friends. Frankly, the outcome was astounding. The fly itself does not appear to have magic powers, but I have reached a point where, when all else fails, I usually take a few fish by tying on one of these streamers. It is simple enough to tie. Here is a description of the pattern:

THE LLAMA

Head: black with white painted eye and black pupil
Tail: grizzly (barred Rock) hackle fibers
Body: red floss, oval tapered
Rib: fine to medium gold tinsel, depending on size of fly
Wing: guard hairs from back of woodchuck
Collar: barred Rock hackle

The hook I use for this pattern is a Mustad 38941 in size 6, 8, or 10. The hook size depends on the length of the guard hairs on the woodchuck. You should be able to obtain the following progression of color change from the wing as it emerges from the head: black, tan, black, and white tips.

The wing is tied straight back over the hook shank, extending as long as the tail, both approximately a quarter of an inch past the hook bend.

For high spring water this fly should be weighted for effectiveness. It can be fished across stream on a dead drift, or stripped and twitched with the rod to produce a darting minnow action. It is one of the few flies I will not go astream without.

Though I have never tied one for myself, Ted Niemeyer, of Connecticut, ties a nymph for the *Isonychia* using the coarse underfur along the leg of the woodchuck for dubbing. You have to find the right-colored animal for this, but if you do, the shade is an effective fiery brown, just right for this pattern. If you use this hairy fur, be sure to use the double-loop method of dubbing in order to lock in the material. It behaves a bit like polar bear and seal fur.

The woodchuck also has some softer, truer dubbing material on its back, just under those guard hairs we've been using. These are a dusty coal black. Need I say more? How often do you find natural black dubbing fur?

I will mention one final pattern in which woodchuck can be used, though this conclusion does not even begin to tell you of the further possibilities inherent in this beautiful fur.

Though I am not a tier of salmon flies, I would highly recommend the 'chuck to those of you who are.

The following pattern was, I believe, originated by Francis Betters, of Wilmington, New York, and it is appropriately named the Au Sable Wulff, since Francis's tackle shop sits almost on the banks of that famed stream:

AU SABLE WULFF

Wing: white calf tail
Body: bleached Australian opossum
Tail: fibers from the tail of a woodchuck
Hackle: brown and grizzly mixed

Au Sable Wulff

Since these chapters are primarily intended to give you an idea of a course to follow, and not necessarily list a great number of patterns, it also follows that to accomplish this purpose, the ideal materials to use for demonstrations would be those that are the most readily accessible, and to show how much variety may be obtained from them.

In almost, though not all, varieties of animal or bird skins, it is possible to make an effective pattern using only the skin of one individual animal. To illustrate my point I will take the common ruffed grouse and offer an imitation of a nymph that will prove effective, without using any fly-tying material other than the hook and thread.

Grouse Nymph

Since this is a nondescript pattern you can give it a name of your own, or simply call it the Grouse Nymph.

GROUSE NYMPH

Tail: fibers from the tail feather of a ruffed grouse (brown)
Body: gray grouse down or fluff tapered
Ribbing: stripped center quill from grouse tail feather, wound in spiral, one next to the other
Thorax: tannish down from base of tail feathers
Legs: grouse body feather tied on its back and folded over
Wing Case: section of fibers from black tip of grouse tail
Head: black

Let's look at the actual construction of this nymph. If you do not have a section of grouse tail and some body feathers, try the same nymph with a mallard duck, using the appropriate parts.

Having placed a hook—either a Mustad Number 3906B or 9671—in your vise, wind on some black thread and spiral it toward the bend.

Take two or three fibers from the tail feather of the grouse and tie them in, angling outward from the hook.

Selecting tail fibers

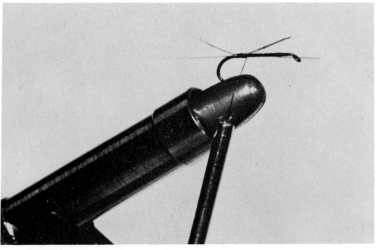

Tying in fibers

Your next step will require some prior preparation; your complete tail feather from the grouse should be allowed to soak overnight in a jar of water. It should be completely submerged in the water, and the jar covered with a lid to prevent the feather from bobbing out. When you're ready to tie the nymph, take the tail feather and lay it down flat on your tying desk. Take a single-edged razor blade and make a nick in the center quill fiber near the tip, loosening a small section of the quill from the main stem. Once you have it started, grasp the loose flap with a pair of tweezers and pull the strip section of quill all the way down the length of the feather.

Nicking center quill with razor

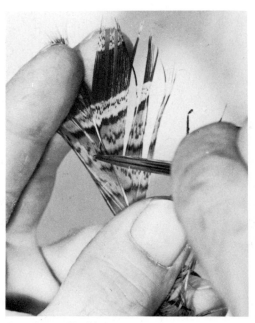

Grasping quill with tweezers

Center quill stripped down

For practical purposes, when making quill strips of this sort, it is best to do them in quantity, let them dry, and then store. Each bird or different feather undergoing this process should have its separate storage. When you are ready to use them, it is simple enough to just soak them, prior to any tying operation.

You now have your stripped quill for the ribbing, which is tied in at the bend of the hook and left idling temporarily.

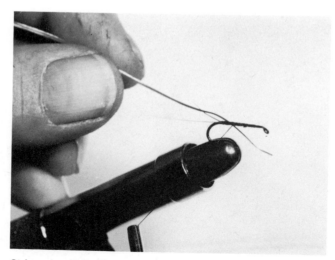

Stripped quill tied in

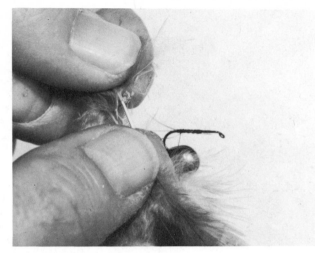

Stripping fluff from feather base

Pick a few of the grouse body feathers, preferably some of those that can be used later for the legs, yet that also have some gray fluff or down adhering to their base. Strip it off, or cut the downy fluff from the feather.

Give your thread a little extra waxing and dub on the grouse down, tapering it so that when you wind toward the thorax area you achieve a natural-looking, cone-shaped body.

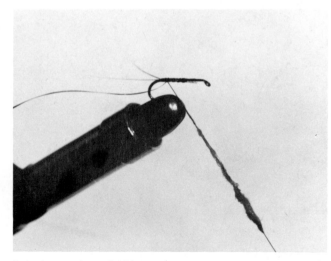

Spinning on down dubbing

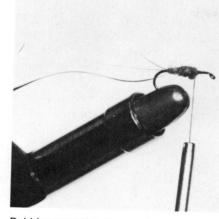

Dubbing wound to thorax

The body should be about two thirds as long as the hook shank. Now go back and grasp the idling, stripped quill, and wind it forward in a natural spiral toward the thread and tie it down.

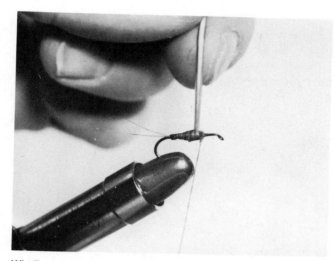

Winding stripped quill to thorax

I would use a touch of head lacquer at this junction to prevent any slippage, since the quill, when dry, will be of smooth texture. A cement will add some strength at this point.

The wing case is now tied in. Take one of the tail feathers from the grouse and snip about an eighth-inch section from the black fibers at the tip end. Since these fibers are relatively thin, as compared with goose or duck, it may be wise to use two of them, one on top of the other, so that when they are pulled forward you will attain the correct density.

Lay them on their backs, with the cut-off section extending toward the bend of the hook, and the dull side facing up, and tie them in at the tips.

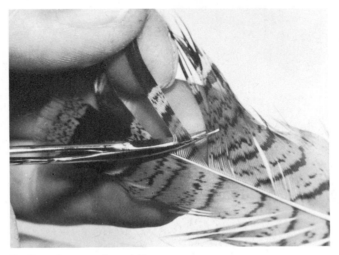

Cutting wing case from tail

Having tied in the wing case, leave it as is, and take one of the body feathers you have defluffed, or any other having the size and coloration needed, and separate the tip from the main fibers that will act as the legs. Lay the feather on its back, butt end toward the bend of the hook, and tie it in at the juncture of fiber separation.

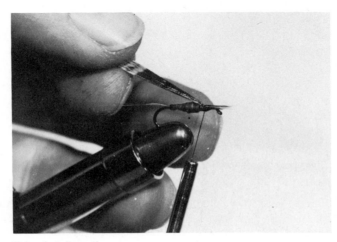

Tying in tail section

Tip separated from main fibers

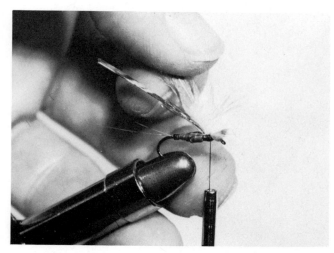

Body feather tied in

To build the thorax, which is your next step, select some of the fluffy down from the base of the whole section of tail feathers, as it comes from the grouse. This down will be of light tan and orange. Spin some onto your thread and form a suitable hump to imitate the thorax as it would appear on the natural nymph. Add fluff as required for correct size.

Thorax tied in

Bring your final turn of thread to a point just before the eye of the hook, grasp the body feather previously tied in, and fold it forward over the thorax, so the fibers, which will become the legs, curve downward. Tie the feather down at the thread point.

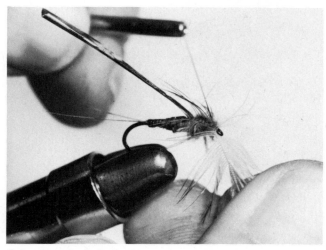

Tying down body feather

Finally, take the wing case section and also fold it over the thorax and body feathers, stroking the latter downward with your fingers, while pulling the wing case taut. Tie in the wing case at the same point as the body feather.

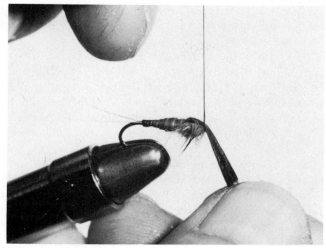

Tying down wing case

Finished grouse nymph

Clip away the excess, whip on a head, and the fly is finished.

For appearances, you may wish to lacquer the wing case with head cement. A number of coatings will give you a more pleasing effect than only one or two. You might also apply a fine coating on the tail fibers, which, on this pattern, are fragile.

Some of the parts of the grouse, which we have used for this pattern, may be interchanged. An example would be the fibers used as the tailing for this nymph. If you wish some that are more durable, pluck a pair of the black feathers, which on the grouse are located between the shoulders and the neck of the bird, and cut the fibers away from the stem. The defibered black stem will be used for your nymph tails. The fuzzy effect left by cutting the fibers will make for effective action.

The wing case may also be made of brown shades from the tail feathers, or blue gray from birds having this shade. Or, if a dark brown wing case is desired, grouse wing-quill feathers may be utilized.

The grouse, one of our more common birds, offers only various shades of brown and gray. Think, then, how much more you would be able to tie with such other game birds as the mallard, wood duck, ringneck pheasant, and so forth, not to mention the readily available domestics, or the more difficult species obtainable in certain regions, yet having a unique color scheme.

This is part of the enjoyment of collecting: to be able to experiment, and hopefully to create our own successful imitations, or improve on the existing ones with materials far more suitable to the purpose.

The Grouse Nymph was not designed as a so-called "killer" pattern. It was created so that you could see what may be done with limited materials at hand, and how to exploit them to the fullest. While it will take fish, I am sure you will be more successful if you use and intermingle the proper materials, whether imitative or suggestive, for the patterns and effects you are searching for.

THE VERSATILE PEACOCK

Light Edson Tiger, Grey Ghost, Supervisor, Silver Darter, **Quill Gordon**, Blue Quill, Grey Hackle, the Coachman family, Alexandra, Alder; streamers, dries, wets, and countless nymphs—what do they have in common? They all use peacock in one form or another, whether for body, topping, legs, feelers, or tails. Use of the common peacock eyed tail and sword is almost limitless.

The following series of nymph patterns will illustrate a few uses of this material you may not have thought of. The first two are submitted by Paul Mead, of Shelburne Falls, Massachusetts.

PEACOCK STEM

Tail: two fibers from underside of peccary
Body: Insect Green floss covered with a bleached, stripped quill from
    stem of peacock tail
Rib: fiber from peccary skin
Thorax: heavy herled peacock quills
Wing Case: brown turkey
Legs: grizzly hen hackle
Head: black

The unusual aspect of this nymph is that the *main stem* of the peacock eyed tail—the part that actually grows out of the bird and is usually discarded after the herled flues have been used—is being utilized.

Preparation for this quill is quite simple. The stem is nicked with a razor blade and stripped down. In this case you don't have to soak the quill first. Any width desired can be cut and stripped. Because some of the pith and thickness of the quill remain after it has been pulled off, it is immersed in a fullstrength solution of Clorox, which will remove the remaining pith, slim it down, and turn it into a clear quill fiber. Used in this manner, the green floss that has been wound for the body of the fly will show through the bleached quill. Because of this translucency the ribbing may also be wound prior to the winding of the stem quill. The latter, because of its strength, will in turn protect both the floss and the ribbing from undue wear.

Peacock Stem

PEACOCK MIDGE NYMPH

Body: blue portion of herl from center of a peacock eye quill—that part closest to stem

Thorax: gold and green portions coming from same flue from peacock eye

Peacock Midge Nymph

This nymph is tied on a number 18 hook. Using the one herl from the center of the "eyed" portion of the peacock tail enables you to obtain a fine diameter for the body since the blue area has very little flue compared to that in the green area. You therefore get a natural taper to form both body and thorax with one simple tying operation. The color change from blue to green to bronze also adds to its effectiveness.

"Woly" Wolyniec of Massapequa, New York, is both a fly-fisherman and an artist, in that order, though his talents are not necessarily ranked in that sequence. He is also a fly-tying instructor with a great deal of patience.

One of his favorite haunts is the Esopus, which originates in the high Catskill peaks and finds its level in the Ashokan reservoir at East Hurley, New York. Woly's familiarity with streamlife in this water created the following pattern. It has been used with highly effective results.

THE ESOPUS BROWN (nymph)

Tail: three short fibers of bronze peacock herl
Body: a 2XL hook (sizes 12 or 14) bent with pliers to form slight "S" shape. Lead wire tied in alongside of hook shank to simulate flat body, over which brown raffia is wound and lacquered.
Wing Case: dark brown turkey or black crow, lacquered
Thorax: three strands of bronze peacock herl
Legs: black hackle
Head: black

Esopus Brown

You will notice that the above pattern calls for *bronze* peacock herl, as do many other imitations. Many tiers when ordering peacock from a supply house stress that they want the "eyed" tail having bronze herl.

All peacock has some bronze shading to it—some more, some less. However, a true bronze peacock tail is scarcer than a natural dun rooster neck. How then can you obtain a true and total bronze effect when a pattern calls for it?

There are two ways—one long, the other short.

(1) The long way is to take a number of peacock sticks and make a floral array of them. Find a window with a good southern exposure and place your bouquet in front of it. Within a year or so you will have some very nice bronzed peacock tails.

(2) The shorter route is to mix up a dyebath using a magenta dye. Any true brand of magenta will do. Soak the peacock as described in the chapter on dyeing and immerse it in the magenta dyebath. Allow it to dry. Fluff it back to shape with steam from the teakettle. Time: One hour.

You may have noticed that I used a bird skin for the experiment of tying one fly only, and your question may be, "What about animals?" Also, I only tied a nymph, to which the grouse was very conducive. You probably cannot tie too many dries with only animal fur.

With a rooster there is an endless list of patterns you can simulate by using the feathers, quills, and hackles of one cock alone. This particular bird would also lend itself to the tying of dry flies very readily.

Furred animals, on the other hand, while they lend themselves to nymphs with no apparent effort, some wets, and some streamers—again all from the same species of game—are not really made for tying the dry fly. Yet even that can be done if you wish to take the trouble of weaving the guard hairs into a hackle.

All, or almost all, animals have guard hairs. They will with no difficulty make wings and tailing for you. The underfur will make the body, which in turn may be ribbed by long guard hairs. To float the fly for dry-fly fishing will depend on the type of animal. If it is a muskrat, the effort will be tedious, since the guard hairs must be clipped from the hide, then aligned horizontally between two taut pieces of tying thread, cemented and twisted into a rope hackle, and trimmed to proper hackle size before they are tied in to form a hackle collar to float the fly.

Other species, such as wild pig, or peccary, may be made to float by utilizing the very stiff body hairs and tying them in as legs, outrigger style, to support the fly on the stream surface. I would not recommend these for fast water, however.

Therefore, if it is possible to tie a fly from the feathers or furs of one species only, the variety and types that may be tied by intermingling, in proper use, leaves a wide-open, unexplored field before you. There is no end.

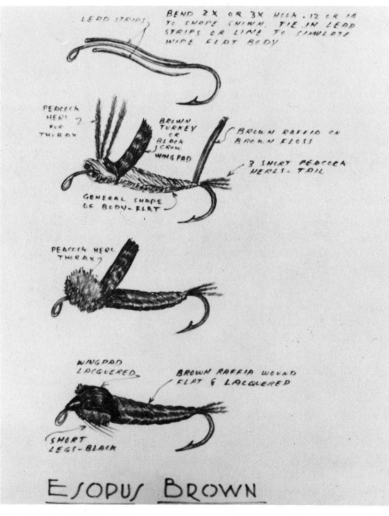

Tying Esopus Brown nymph

HACKLELESS FLIES

Most of you are aware that a very successful book, of recent vintage, has been published regarding the use of flies that are tied to float without the use of hackle. The name of this book is *Selective Trout* by Doug Swisher and Carl Richards, and it expounds the theory of permitting a dry fly to alight on the stream surface, keeping the body and wings of the fly closer to a trout's eye view. I highly recommend this work to you because it has its place, especially when fishing some of the slower streams where trout may rise slowly and inspect your offering with great selectivity.

There are many streams and many pools in many streams that meet the demands of this type of fly. It was not intended for fast water, or the large broiling streams indigenous to certain sections of the country. The traditionalists among us can be assured that the standard dry flies will not be replaced, and we will still have our Cahills, Gordons, and Wulffs. The hackleless flies are a supplement designed to fill a gap and should be part of your gear when you take to the river, on the chance that an occasion may arise when you will find a need for them.

Since the book has been published there have been a rash of sales, by mail-order houses, of hen necks. The reason for this is that the soft and webby fibers of the hen neck are ideally suited for the soft fluffy wing, which will silhouette beautifully for the trout, and settle on the water like a piece of thistledown.

I would like to expand on this theory just a little. While hen necks are excellent for the hackleless wing, they are not the only, or the best, kind of material for this fly. Duck or goose feathers, especially in the required shades and in their natural state, are excellent.

Duck and goose, as you will recall, resist water. You will have found this out if you've tried to submerge some for dyeing, and watched them bob up, again and again, like corks. The plumage of these birds has a built-in buoyancy which, if you are tying flies designed to float without hackle, is highly desirable. They are also all web and silhouette in the proper manner.

Unfortunately, all of us cannot always obtain all the species of duck we would like to add to our collections, due mainly to their varying migratory routes. This is where your surplus trading material can be used to advantage. From coast to coast certain species are more common as game in one area than they are in another. Take a look at one of the books on birds of North America and you will notice how many kinds of ducks there are.

With few exceptions, the shades needed for the tying of hackleless patterns may be had in their natural color, if you obtain the appropriate duck. If not, the breast plumage can be dyed to the proper hue, though it will lose some of its natural oils in the dyeing process.

For a complete color range, without the use of dyeing processes, you would have to go to other wild or domestic members of the bird family. Recently I received from a friend in Arizona, Chandler Smith, a fly tied from the feathers of the California quail. It was a hackleless fly, beautifully done, and perfectly matched in shade. Now, most of us are not in a position to obtain the California quail, which is indigenous to the Southwest. Again, if you know anyone in the region, and you happen to live in Connecticut, offer him a common merganser in trade for the quail, and you will both benefit.

You can use the feathers from any bird for hackleless flies, provided it performs in the manner of the hen hackle.

A short while ago I asked Doug Swisher why he was using rabbit fur on the body of many of the hackleless flies mentioned in *Selective Trout*. The answer was, availability and the ability to dye white rabbit to the desired shade. He agreed that certain other furs were preferable, especially those of water animals, such as beaver and muskrat. The problem was that these latter could not be dyed as easily, or at all to certain desired shades, unless they were bleached first. I concur. Yet, some of the shades could be obtained with a little experimentation, and all colors can be attained by the method of first bleaching and then dyeing. This last process, as I mentioned before, is not too desirable, since the dual operation takes away the natural oils and luster of the fur. However, if there is no other recourse, then by all means use the dual process.

Incidentally, beaver and muskrat can be dyed into all of the darker hues as they are. For this you will have to use the underbelly of these animals, which is lighter in shade. I have had success with such colors as olive, brown, blue, and red. Some of the shades, because they are not quite true, prove quite interesting.

The rabbit, while a fine dubber, is not desirable for dry flies simply because he soaks up water like a sponge. A little research is in order, and if undertaken, the purpose of the hackleless fly, as introduced by Doug Swisher and Carl Richards in *Selective Trout,* can only be advanced that much further.

PATTERNS YOU MAY NOT HAVE TIED

The following are little-known patterns, though they may have been tied in similar form by some of you. I list them because they have proven effective for me and hopefully will accomplish the same purpose for you when you wet your line.

CONDOR QUILL NYMPH

Tail: dark ginger hackle fibers tied short

Underbody: two pieces of medium lead wire tied in, one along each side of hook shank, with ends toward bend tapered to shank with razor blade

Body: stripped condor dyed yellow, or stripped center quill of mallard duck dyed yellow, edge marked with brown

Thorax: peacock herl

Wing Case: speckled brown turkey wing quill

Legs: red game or dark ginger hackle fibers

Head: black

The above fly was originated by Leo Runkowski of Massapequa, New York, and is also tied with a green body, using the same quill material. It has a flat shape and, being weighted, rides low in the water.

Condor Quill Nymph

On Leo's wall there is a beautiful four-and-one-half pound rainbow, taken from one of the feeder streams of the Esopus, to attest to the fly's effectiveness. Though I can boast of none of such size, this small nymph has taken its share of trout for me in my own endeavors. It is tied in sizes 10, 12, and 14.

THE SPIRIT OF PITTSFORD MILLS

Wings: grizzly hackle tips tied in **V** position
Tail: a cream ginger hackle tip tied to proper proportion
Body: down from base of wood duck flank feather
Rib: cream ginger hackle, wound Palmer style and clipped short to
    blend in with body. Stubby effect.
Hackle: cream ginger

Most of you are familiar with the above fly, but the version here submitted by Dave Kashner, of the Orvis Company, is tied slightly differently.

The fly, as Dave informs me, is named after the town of Pittsford Mills, in Vermont, through which a small stream called Furnace Brook meanders on into the beautiful Green Mountains. The waters of this freestone stream harbor a strain of rainbow trout that is not migratory—an unusual occurrence. Though seldom exceeding fourteen inches in length, these trout are reputed to be among the wildest, thus making for some exciting dry-fly fishing.

The body of the above fly can also be tied with creamy kapok, a substitute which may float better in the faster waters. Twelve and fourteen are the most popular sizes.

Spirit of Pittsford Mills

THE CROW

Tail: fibers from short tail of ringneck pheasant
Underbody: two strips of lead wire tapered to hook shank and tied, one along each side to thorax
Body: yellow wool, marked with brown (use Magic Marker) on topside, and scraped to create fuzzy effect on underside
Rib: stripped center quill from secondary wing quill of crow, or center quill stripped from tail feather
Legs: partridge hackle
Wing Case: quarter-inch section of crow wing fibers, lacquered
Thorax: three heavy herled peacock quills tied in simultaneously to effectual diameter
Head: black, large

The above pattern is a favorite imitation used by Gus Nevros, who originated it. The rib of stripped crow may be tied in an open spiral to allow the fuzzy, yellow wool to show from underneath this nymph, or it can be tied in touching wraps to present an all-black yet segmented body. Both are effective.

It is tied on a Mustad 9672 hook in sizes ten and twelve.

The Crow

THE VARIANT

Tail: cree hackle fibers
Body: center quill from Rhode Island Red rooster
Hackle: cree
Head: black

This simple pattern, tied without wings, is one pattern without which Harold Campbell, of New York City, will not go upstate.

Many of his flies are tied without wings, and I don't know whether it is because he does not like to tie wings, or simply that he does so well in taking fish with his favorite pattern.

This pattern is tied with a dark cree hackle, but many of the imitations in this fisherman's vest range from the lightest to the darkest of variants, and hackles from the necks of breeds, especially flecked or spotted roosters. Frankly, I can't argue against the simplicity of this pattern. I've taken too many trout with it myself.

It is tied from sizes 12 down to 22.

An egg sac pattern you may wish to try is one tied by **Ted Niemeyer.** Its uniqueness is in its simplicity. The method used in tying female imitations of the natural can be used in other patterns calling for the use of an egg sac. Ted's description is as follows:

The Variant

NIEMEYER EGG SAC

Hook: Mustad No. 94837 in sizes 10, 12, 14
Tail: dark blue dun hackle
Body: dubbed muskrat
Hackle: one dark grizzly and one dark blue dun hackle feather mixed
Wing: none
Sac: hackle butt or duck breast stem (hollow stem taken from rooster, duck, or other suitable bird) dipped three times in fluorescent enamel in this order. White, then let dry, orange, and finally fluorescent yellow.

The hollow stem from a hackle or duck feather is, of course, an ideal floatant. It is tied in along the top of the hook shank so that the bulb portion, which has been enameled, extends just past the bend of the hook shank.

Niemeyer Egg Sac

All other materials are tied in using standard procedures.

One final pattern I will list is of local origin. It is tied by Vince Stayter of Croton-on-Hudson, New York. The neighboring area contains such streams as the Amawalk, Croton, and the West Branch of the Croton, not to mention innumerable ponds and lakes that harbor not only most varieties of trout, but also bass, pickerel, and panfish.

The pattern submitted has not only proved effective over quite a number of years, but also under extremely adverse conditions at times. It may be due to the one unusual ingredient contained in this particular imitation. Here is the pattern:

THE MOUSE HAIR SPECIAL (dry)

Wing: slate gray mallard wing quills, tied divided
Tail: badger hackle fibers having a black list
Body: white-footed deer mouse fur; all fur including small guard hairs
    are dubbed in
Hackle: brown and badger mixed
Head: black

Actually, though I knew the fur of the common field mouse made excellent dubbing material, I was quite unaware of the species called the "white-footed deer mouse," although I have probably seen it a number of times while out deer hunting. They are found where you find pine trees, dwelling mostly in leaf nests on the ground.

The Mouse Hair Special (dry)

Vince's recommendation for their capture consists of setting out the small conventional mousetraps baited with peanut butter. I'm told that besides the mice you will also obtain a certain percentage of shrews, also an excellent addition to your materials supply.

Do not be concerned with the germ- or disease-carrying vermin usually associated with rodents when pursuing these creatures in the wild. They are cleaner than most house pets.

The fur on the white-footed deer mouse has brownish red overtones; it is not pure gray.

11 Synthetic Materials and Patterns

I would be remiss if I did not include in a volume dealing with fly-tying materials patterns utilizing not only the natural supplies that come from birds or animals, but many of the manufactured variety; in recent years these have become an important part of the flytier's arsenal.

Though mail-order houses are very much like the five and dime stores, in that they carry every size, color, and shape of the numerous materials available to meet the tier's needs, I suspect they are sometimes driven to distraction when a new article appears in some outdoor publication or fly-fisherman's quarterly in which the author has presented a new or substitute pattern with some unique fiber or material.

If the article and the fly are successful, the item in question is then usually bought wholesale by your supply house and resold through that channel to you. Like yourself, I have many times paused at various counters in our local five and dime and wondered as to the possibilities of odds and ends that could be used on a fly. Here again, the exploration, and exploitation, is an endless crusade, not only because of the seemingly limitless items now available, but also those new ones that are constantly being created and manufactured.

I do not know which tier first learned of the use of Mylar tubing, but I do know that it was not originally manufactured for the express purpose of the flytier, though many of us have come to accept it for just that purpose alone. It was designed for millinery purposes, to be used in the making of garments, draperies, and other such "remote" things. Nevertheless, it has a permanent place with us.

Mylar, Phentex (polypropylene), and Mohlon yarn, and certain cements are of fairly recent vintage. These are but a few of the many synthetic materials, now listed in books on fly tying, that have made the scene in our fraternity.

It is therefore only natural that we look into a few of these and list their uses as far as some of the more recent patterns are concerned. Used correctly, these materials have made certain imitations much more effective than they were before. They are also responsible for some of the newer original patterns.

MYLAR is a metallic, yet soft, synthetic fiber that comes in large sheets, which are usually gold on one side and silver on the other. In this form the material can be cut into strips of desired size and used as a flaring attractor, or if tied as a ribbing, can be used either as gold or silver.

Mylar also comes in braided form of various diameters, in both silver and gold, though here the colors are not intermingled. The sizes most commonly used by flytiers are one-sixteenth, one-eighth, and three-sixteenths of an inch in diameter.

Braided Mylar is customarily used in the making of a body on a streamer fly. The very fact that it is braided gives it a scaly appearance, not unlike the natural minnow it imitates. It may also be fished in both fresh and salt water without fear of tarnishing or rusting. In addition, it is lighter in weight without sacrificing relative strength. All these attributes are advantages over the standard tinsel, though this latter will always remain a part of fly tying. Tinsel, as such, also has some advantages over Mylar.

To make the body of a streamer fly, the braided Mylar is simply decored. The substance used as a core on this material is usually a few strands of string or yarn twisted together, and thus manufactured in order to retain the oval shape of the Mylar braiding. Once this filler has been removed, the tubelike Mylar can be slipped over the eye of the hook and be bound down at both tail and fore end.

To add shape, another synthetic is first tied onto the hook shank and given proper dimension according to the tier's preference, prior to sliding on the now-hollow Mylar tubing. The usual filler here is a type of synthetic called Curon. It is spongy, soft, elastic, and adhering, and is thus easily stretched and pulled to any shape needed.

The streamer fly of this type may be further enhanced by the addition of a coat of varnish; this is allowed to dry, and then spots or stripes are painted upon it, furthering the imitation theory for minnows and bait fish. Flies of this type have been tied from a small size ten to saltwater flies in sizes 3/o, 4/o, and 5/o.

The following pattern, used first for salt water, may also be used in certain freshwater streamers or bucktails. It is basic in design, but incorporates the use of braided Mylar.

MYLAR BUCKTAIL

> *Hook:* Mustad No. 3407 in sizes 1/o, 2/o
> *Body:* silver tinsel
> *Wing:* white bucktail over which are strands from braided Mylar tubing, over which is light blue bucktail, all about three inches long
> *Throat:* short tuft of red bucktail
> *Head:* red thread, lacquered

The unique use of Mylar on the above pattern is that a piece of braided Mylar tubing is decored, and with the point of a dubbing needle, the interwoven strands of Mylar are unbraided, strand by strand, until the desired length is reached. These separate and loose strands have a twist to them, which is left as is, and they are tied in as if they were hair. Action, light refraction, and attraction are the intended use of Mylar in this form.

Mylar Bucktail

The above pattern is sometimes varied in color as far as the bucktail wing is concerned. Most tiers prefer the blue top wing, but occasionally a light green, red, or yellow topping proves a superior fish-taker.

Destranded Mylar tubing can be used in such freshwater attractor bucktails as the Mickey Finn, or in the imitative, such as the Black-nosed Dace. They will create flash when stripped through the water imitating a darting minnow, and this is the intent of this form of usage. Hook preference and pattern type remain the same, except for the addition of the Mylar.

Although polypropylene yarn was first introduced to most of you through the Swisher-Richards book, I had received a sample dry fly from a tier in Canada, tying with this material, a year prior to the publication of the book. Foolishly I overlooked its potential at the time.

What makes polypropylene, having the trade name of Phentex, a desirable, is its specific gravity to water. I believe it is actually 94 percent the weight of water, and therefore lighter, making it an excellent floatant, especially for the bodies of dry flies. This subject has been adequately covered in *Selective Trout*. It does and should not end there, however, as I discovered through my inquisitive fishing buddy Bob Sater, who thought it would make a very good imitation of the Black Ant, a terrestrial pattern, and one which he forthwith proceeded to tie—and take fish with!

POLYPROPYLENE BLACK ANT

Hook: Mustad No. 94833 or Orvis Premium fine wire
Body: stranded black polypropylene yarn wound in forming two distinct bodies
Hackle: two turns of black hackle at waist
Head: black thread, smaller than bodies

The pattern is easy enough to tie. The only trouble you may encounter is in the building of the two humps to shape the ant and this is due to the slippery, smooth texture of this yarn. To overcome this, simply take a turn of thread over the yarn when it has been raised to the point where it begins to slide.

Polypropylene Black Ant

With the light wire hook, tied in sizes 14 through 20, and the use of the buoyant Phentex, the Ant will ride very nicely in the surface film.

Another use for this fine new synthetic would be the Inchworm pattern. Many types, from chenille to deer hair, are tied. Some float, and some do not. The one made of polypropylene, tied on an Orvis Superfine hook will, as with the Ant, ride in the surface film.

INCHWORM

Body: polypropylene yarn wound full, not tapered, to size of natural inchworm. Shade, light green.
Rib: green thread spiraled through body tautly to form segmented natural bulges
Head: two turns of peacock herl tied off with black thread

When trout start gorging themselves in June on this morsel, try the above imitation. Using a fine tippet will help.

Inchworm

Have you ever had the problem of trying to taper the body of the Quill Gordon dry pattern, prior to wrapping on the peacock quill, without adding weight to the fly? Try tying this old standby in the following manner:

QUILL GORDON (dry)

Wing: wood duck flank
Tail: blue dun hackle
Underbody: lemon yellow Phentex yarn tapered to wing
Body: stripped peacock eye herl
Hackle: blue dun

Besides adding to the floatability of the fly, the yellow underbody will allow some of its color to glow through the stripped peacock quill for a more natural appearance.

Polypropylene comes in many shades and can be used to advantage on many other patterns.

Quill Gordon

MOHLON, while also a water-resistant floatant material, has been more widely publicized for use on fuzzy nymphs in the book by Polly Roseborough, *Tying and Fishing the Fuzzy Nymph.*

It is indeed fuzzy and would not seem to be preferred on some of our dry flies, requiring a smoother and more streamlined body. Yet it is the only material I use for tying the body of the Black Gnat dry. If you have not tried it, here is the pattern description for this imitation, using the synthetic acrylic orlon called Mohlon.

> *BLACK GNAT (dry)*
>
> *Wing:* mallard duck quill, slate gray
> *Tail:* black hackle fibers
> *Body:* single-strand Mohlon tapered to wing
> *Hackle:* black hackle fibers
> *Head:* black

Mohlon can be stranded. There are two separate strands entwined as a unit on this yarn. Since it is fuzzy, it will tend to fray and try to get away from you during the tying operation. A little moisture applied to your fingertips will assist you in making it behave properly as you wind and taper it prior to tying it down.

As with Phentex, Mohlon should also be considered for possible use on all quill-bodied flies, whether for dries or nymphs. In the latter case, certain patterns may be improved if the Mohlon underbody is allowed to extend through the ribbing of the quill body by winding the particular quill in a slightly open spiral. This imparts more movement to the imitation.

Black Gnat

One of the tying procedures that has always fascinated me is the art of weaving bodies for the imitation of nymphs. I recently had the good fortune to observe Ralph Graves, of the Southern New York Fish and Game Association, tie one of his now famous, flat-bodied, two-toned nymphs, using as the body material two shades of monofilament line. One was yellow, the other brown. When he had completed the fly the brown mono was all on the back of the nymph and the yellow formed the underbelly. The imitation was flat, as most emergers tend to be, but in addition, due to the weaving, there was a lifelike segmentation on each side of the body.

To attain this effect, Ralph ties two strands of monofilament, about fourteen-pound test, along the sides of the hook shank, binding them down well, and cementing. The continuing strands of mono extend well past the rear of the hook bend by about ten inches.

With the yellow strand on one side and the brown on the other, he brings both of them under the shank of the hook and forms, but does not close, a simple overhand knot with them. Which color is to be on top, and which forms the bottom of the nymph, determines how the loop is made. It is then brought forward from under, and along the bottom of the hook shank to the eye of the hook, and the loop in the overhand knot is opened enough to allow it to slip over the eye, one strand above, and one below, according to color, and pushed back toward the bend where it is pulled taut.

The procedure is repeated until the thorax area is reached; then the other necessary materials are tied in to complete the nymph. The pattern description for Ralph's nymph is:

RALPH'S NYMPH

Tail: two fibers of condor quill (substitute goose quill, dark)
Underbody: lead wire along top of hook shank
Body: alternate yellow and brown strands of monofilament, woven so

that the brown is on top and yellow forms the underside
Thorax: yellow chenille
Wing Case: dark brown turkey, doubled and folded
Legs: two strips of condor (or goose)
Feelers: two strips of condor (or goose)
Eyes: fine brown chenille, with fold of turkey wing case over them.
Lacquered.

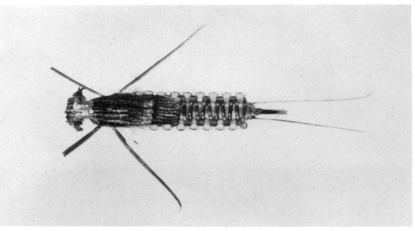

Ralph's Nymph

For methods of tying in the wing case and eyes of this nymph, see the procedures used and photographed for the stonefly nymph, which will be the next pattern covered.

Vinyl cement was first introduced to me by John Mickievicz of Jack's Tackle in Phoenixville, Pennsylvania. For certain purposes, this particular lacquer has a decided advantage over the conventional head cements. John uses it almost exclusively on all his flies, though its primary function is to lacquer wing cases on nymphs.

The purpose of cementing the wing case is, first, to hold the fibers of the material together, to prevent splitting and breaking while being tied in, and later during use on the stream. Its second purpose is to give the necessary glossy appearance where it is called for, especially on some of the hardbacks.

When ordinary, or standard head lacquer is used, the result, though glossy, is of a hard and brittle texture after the cement has dried. Vinyl cement, on the other hand, after drying, leaves the wing case in a stronger, firmer, yet more pliable state. It is of a soft hardness, or, if you prefer, a hard softness. In any case, it does not chip readily, and when used on such materials as turkey or goose, it cements the fibers in a superior manner, while allowing them to have some "give," as in the natural.

The following stonefly, tied by John, will illustrate the use of vinyl cement. You will also notice that he uses a few other manufactured items in this imitation, not too commonly used on the average fly.

STONEFLY

Tail: two fibers of golden pheasant tail
Underbody: fine lead wire
Body: sulfur yellow wool, wound and tapered to thorax
Rib: condor strip, or center strip of light-colored gray goose primary
Legs: body feather from ringneck pheasant (church window)
Wing Case: one-quarter-inch section of light brown turkey wing
Thorax: light yellow (pale) cotton chenille
Eyes: fine brown chenille

In the tying of this pattern, a 6XL hook, such as the Mustad No. 9575, or 3665A is used. Either yellow or brown Monocord can be used for the tying thread, since both will blend in with the color scheme on the overall pattern. I use yellow.

Having affixed your hook in the vise, spiral your thread onto it from the front to the bend of the hook shank. Select two fibers from the tail feather of the golden pheasant. These fibers have a very distinct marking. Tie one in on each side of the hook. Cement the juncture of the tail fibers with a touch of vinyl cement.

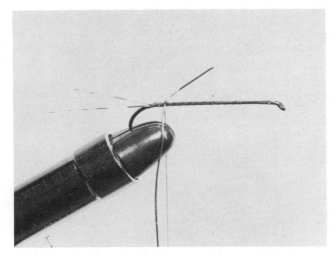

Pheasant fibers and wire tied in

Tying down lead wire

Next take a strip of fine lead wire, approximately three to four inches long, and tie it in slightly above the tail, measuring one end of it, so that when folded, it will extend to about the thorax area. Bend the wire so that there is a strip lining each side of the hook shank, and wrap the tying thread over it to secure it to the thorax area. With the longer part of the wire, make adequate turns around the hook shank rearward to the center of the hook shank. Snip away excess so that the cut portion is on the top side.

Lacquer the wire well and twist the thread through it, returning the thread toward the space between the tail and the tie-in point of the wire.

If you have a strip of condor, tie in the narrow section at the space above the bend of the hook. If condor is no longer available to you, soak and strip a center quill from either a light goose or duck quill for the purpose and tie it in. Let it lie idle.

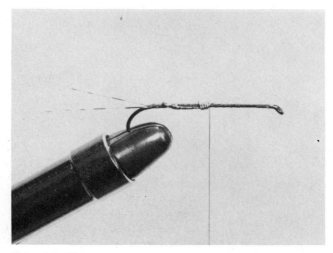

Tying in quill

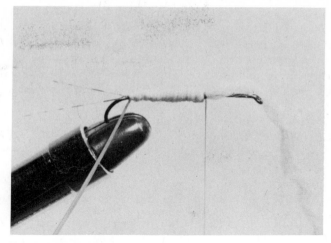

Tying down wool

Take about a ten-inch length of light yellow or sulfur-colored wool and tie it in at the same space the quill was tied in. Keep the short, or butt, end on top of the hook shank and along it up to the thorax area, thus preventing unnecessary bulging. Wrap the wool in a taper toward your thread at the thorax area, forming a slight taper while doing so. Then tie it down.

Now take a Magic Marker, brown shade, and paint the top side of the wool to obtain a two-toned effect.

With a pair of flat-nosed pliers, press the body to a flat shape, in case some of the lead wire has become twisted around while tying in the wool. A gentle pressure will suffice to simulate more closely the proportions of the natural.

Paint the dull underside of your stripped quill with vinyl cement and wrap the quill in close spirals toward the thorax area and tie it down well.

Winding quill to thorax

Snip a quarter-inch section from a light shade of mottled brown turkey wing quill. Try to find a fairly large quill since you will need a bit of length in making this wing case. Apply vinyl cement to the underside of the wing case section about three quarters of an inch downward. Tie in at the tip. The reason for not cementing the whole quill section at once is that it will harden before you are through with it, and you will need a little liquid softness to work with later.

Select a body feather from a ringneck pheasant that is referred to as a "church window" feather. This feather comes from the back of the cock bird near the area of the shoulders of the wings. It has a mottled dark brown and tan center, rimmed by a section of creamy shading, then a black or very dark brown, followed by a light brown contour.

Separate the tip from the body section and tie in at the tip, bottom side up. Apply some cement at this tie-in point.

Tying in wing case

Tying in body feather

For the thorax tie in some cotton chenille of a creamy yellow color. Build the thorax a little longer than average, and slightly higher than the body.

Having left the thread hanging where the thorax was tied in, bring the pheasant body feather forward so it folds over, and thus will form the legs; then tie it down near the eye of the hook. Approximately one sixteenth of an inch should be left between the thorax and the eye of the hook for tying in the "eyes" of the nymph.

Tying in chenille thorax

Tying down body feather

Lay a five-inch section of fine brown chenille across the hook shank at the area between the thorax and the hook eye. Tie it down with a figure eight, as you would a wing on a dry fly.

Tying in fine brown chenille

Apply a little more vinyl cement to the wing case, which has been waiting its turn, bring it forward over the legs, thorax, and chenille, and tie it down with two turns of thread to keep it in place.

Tying down wing case

Now grasp the ends of the brown chenille and tie this material into a simple overhand knot.

Apply another touch of vinyl to the turkey wing case, to keep it soft, and bring it backward over the brown chenille. As soon as the wing case has humped back over the chenille take a few turns of thread around it at this juncture.

Grasp the wing case section at the butt with your right hand and, with your left, place a dubbing needle against the section so that you can double it. Measure so that it will be about one half the size of the full wing case.

Tying knot in chenille

Hold the doubled wing case down with your right thumb and forefinger and bring the thread over the section with your left, using the bobbin. Having secured your doubled wing case, snip away the excess butt.

Apply some cement to the brown chenille protruding from between the folds of the wing case at that junction.

Doubling wing case

Doubled wing case tied down

Clip **excess** brown chenille from wing case, leaving small stubs. These will be your "eyes." Apply vinyl.

Whip finish in front of "eyes" of nymph.

Apply vinyl cement on top sides of wing case if glossy appearance is desired.

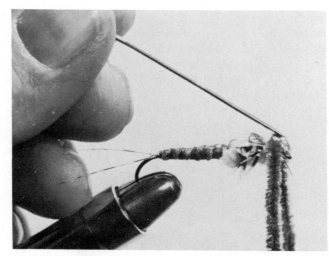

Cementing chenille

Clipping chenille to form "eyes"

Finished stonefly nymph

Incidentally, this method of making the eyes of nymphs need not be restricted to the use of chenille alone. Another synthetic for making excellent "eyes" is monofilament. A good example would be the following pattern, which also incorporates another synthetic, namely the common polyethylene bag.

GRASS SHRIMP

Tail: olive gray hackle tip
Body: olive and gray seal fur palmered with olive gray saddle hackle
Shell: polyethylene bag strip
Rib: greenish monofilament
Eyes: monofilament burned to form small ball on each end
Thread: olive Monocord, or nylon

The tail is tied in first. Following that, and in this order, tie in the ribbing (about eight-pound-test green monofilament will do), then a triangular strip from a poly bag measuring approximately one-quarter inch at one end and tapering to three-eighths inch at the other (tie in narrow end); and lastly, tie in a long olive gray saddle hackle.

Grass Shrimp

All these materials are left idling at the bend of the hook while the seal-fur body is dubbed on, using the double loop method, and wound forward. This accomplished, the saddle hackle is palmered forward, and the poly bag strip is folded over the saddle hackle, forcing it downward and thus forming the legs and the shell simultaneously.

After the poly strip has been tied down near the head, the ribbing of monofilament is brought forward in an open spiral to simulate the natural segmentation of the shrimp.

To form the "eyes," take a short piece of monofilament and apply a lighted match to each end and burn it down so that only an eighth of an inch or so, depending on hook size, remains. You will notice, because it has been burned, that a small ball has formed at each end. Tie this unit in front of the last tie-down point which secured the poly bag strip, using the normal figure eight method, and you will have your protruding "eyes."

Whip-finish an olive head with the thread and the Grass Shrimp is completed.

The hook to use on this pattern should be of a short shank variety and slightly bent, to give the shrimp its natural curve. This can be done with a pair of pliers.

Though basically a saltwater imitation, the pattern can be tied for freshwater scud as well. If the natural shrimp differs in water you fish, simply adjust body color of imitation.

To prove its effectiveness, Bob Sater, whose backyard is Long Island Sound, recently took a four-pound, eight-and-one-half-ounce weakfish with it one summer's evening early this year. Needless to say it was taken with a fly rod.

The foregoing pattern was designed as a direct imitative, using as a guide the common grass shrimp found in coastal waters.

Vinyl cement is also recommended for the Grass Shrimp pattern.

A final tip on the use of vinyl cement. When making dry flies, such as the Quill Gordon, Light Cahill, or Dark Hendrickson, apply a touch of this cement at the base of the divided wing. It firms them up, and keeps them durable and separated.

One random tip John Mickievicz has to offer, in addition to his experimentation with some unique materials, is the use of a common household item called Scotchgard. This spray is used primarily by women to give a protective coating to furniture, ornaments, and other appropriate objects. This protective coating, if sprayed on dry flies after they have been tied, and prior to taking them astream, will act as a water repellent of superior quality, outlasting some of the more commonly used floatants.

Scotchgard is not intended, however, for use on the stream since it requires drying time, and the containers are much too large and bulky to carry in your vest and still have room for the other sundries. It is just an additional aid to the normal silicone solutions.

The foregoing are but a few of the newer synthetic products at our disposal, and like the natural materials, there is a limitless supply of them for our further research and use.

12 Jungle Fowl, Other Departed Species—and Their Substitutes

The waxlike nail feathers from the cape of a jungle cock seem almost irreplaceable. They have been with us for a long, long time, and their use is scarcely limited to a few patterns. All of us will miss them when our existing supplies of this beautiful bird have been used up in our last Gray Ghost or Jassid.

But there is a ban on the importation of these skins from India, the country to which they are supposedly indigenous. India has placed the gray jungle fowl on the protected list. This has been in effect since 1967. The United States, and later Canada and the British Isles, recognized India's protection of this species in 1969. After March of that year it was no longer permissible for anyone to import these skins, whether from India or elsewhere. Existing supplies in this country were allowed to be sold—but by now they are just about gone. What then to tie with for the cheek on the Gray Ghost in the future, or for any other pattern calling for its use?

I would rather tie without the jungle cock eye than use a plastic imitation. My only other alternative is to use a substitute, and while substitutes may not replace the real thing, they can come close if you use a little ingenuity.

Quite a few available birds are suited for this purpose. Some of the obvious ones are the body feathers of a well-marked starling, with its pointed spots of yellowish white. Another source is the neck feathers of various quail, including the bobwhite, though some of our western varieties, such as the California and scaled quail, would be more desirable.

A domestic feather could be the plumage of the common guinea hen, with its white-dotted, black feathers. All of these, when used, would first have to be lacquered to achieve the waxy finish of the natural jungle cock eye. Some may have to be dyed a pale orange yellow first, and then lacquered.

One of the recent substitutions suggested to me by Ted Niemeyer was a feather I do not often use, and yet have quite a few of—the barred black and white flank feather of the wood duck. Select one of these feathers, lacquer it with clear varnish, and tie it in as you would the original.

Here now you have a few replacements for this endangered species. The sad part about the whole affair is that while all of us, as sportsmen, would rather not tie with any species that is endangered, the fate of the jungle cock is rather questionable. Although Indian laws prohibit its exportation, its skins are still being collected by natives, after the bird has been killed for food, and are either being stockpiled in that country for future sale, or are even now being sold to countries that do not prohibit its importation. We can only hope that they are given a chance to recover and may again be legitimately harvested.

Besides the jungle fowl, there are other birds either on the endangered species list or simply unobtainable due to importation laws prohibiting their entry into this country. In any event, we will list those that are no longer, or no longer will be, obtainable and suggest possible substitutions for their usage. Also included will be the skins of some of the more difficult, though legal, feathers to obtain.

CONDOR. Prohibited. Closest available substitute: large, natural gray, goose wing quills.

CONDOR (STRIPPED). Stripped peacock. Stripped center quill from certain geese, duck, and turkey feathers having brown segmentation at their edge. Plain white stripped quills from same birds, painted for segmentation and lacquered.

LAND RAIL. This is the feather from one of the English birds of this species. I have only seen one sample feather, and it appears to be of a mottled light orange tan hue. The closest suggestions for its substitution are from quills from a mottled cinnamon turkey tail or wing; light hen mallard side feathers, or some of the flank from a cinnamon teal, though this latter bird will be difficult for most of us to obtain.

PLOVER. In England called the golden plover. The breast of this bird is of a dun cast, and the back a dark gray dun. If you are familiar with the freshwater coot, sometimes called mudhen, its feathers may be used as a substitute.

WOODCOCK (ENGLISH). Grouse, sparrow, woodcock. The markings are not as exact as the English variety, but make a close substitute.

KINGFISHER and/or BLUE CHATTERER. The unique coloration of these birds is difficult to duplicate. I would suggest the McGinty feather of the mallard duck, if that could be lightened in shade. Most substitutions for these birds will have to be of the dyed variety, usually from the quills of young, white domestic duck.

PARTRIDGE (ENGLISH). All grouse native to the United States come close, if not at times duplicating it.

SNIPE. White and gray pigeon.

DOTTEREL. Secondary or undercovert of English starling wings.

BALI DUCK. Though many feathers of this beautiful bird are not easily duplicated, the various sections of such ducks as teal, widgeon, and pintail may be substituted. None, however, has either the triple-striped "Jess Wood" streamer feather, or the delicate blue-barred side feather, though this latter can be dyed, using mallard flank.

SWAN. Domestic white goose.

TETRUS PHEASANT. Turkey, medium dark brown speckled.

SCARLET IBIS. Though rarely used today, with the exception of some salmon flies, it can be duplicated by the dyeing to that shade of pale, yet firm red, the breast feathers of the wood duck.

WOOD DUCK FLANK. Mallard flank dyed a lemon brown.

There are, of course, a multitude of feathers from the skins of birds that are no longer available. Most of them I have never had the pleasure of even seeing, much less working with. To have seen and used some of these materials would make the task of suggested substitutions much simpler. However, the plumage of some of the protected and rare species is no longer listed in recent books on fly tying, and where they were listed, the work was usually by an English author, describing the dressing of patterns we are unlikely to use in our own streams.

Hopefully, the few lines regarding substitutions will be of some help in certain cases. Basically, the most important thought to keep in mind is that which I have mentioned before, and that is *to be able to arrive at the desired imitation, whether directly imitative or suggestive, use the available materials in the proper manner, and those most suited for the pattern.*

13 Sources of Supply— Mail Order, Retail

For the most part, the success of any mail-order establishment depends primarily on quality, service, and the sale of items not commonly found in local outlets. All reputable mail-order houses are aware of these essentials, and will do their best to meet these obligations, since it is just plain good business.

As far as fly-tying materials go, there are quite a few mail-order companies in existence, though not all of them advertise as extensively as others. This may be due to the fact that these exceptions have reached what they feel to be a capacity, or substantial, mailing list, and are not seeking further expansion. Most of these concerns, besides listing fly-tying materials, will also catalog such related items as rod-building equipment, fly rods, reels, lines, and associated commodities. Some are geared for fly tying, and carry the other goods as an additional source of revenue, while the reverse may be true with those companies highlighting finished products such as pretied flies, lures, fishing vests, and all the gadgets that can be stuffed into or hung from them.

Though all of these companies will carry identical basic materials, they will vary in certain categories in style, sizes, color, or specialize in certain feathers or furs some other companies either do not have a source for or find their wholesale cost too prohibitive. Everyone runs his ship the way he sees fit. I urge you to send away for all the mail-order catalogs so that you may read them at your leisure and see what each has to offer.

You will find that prices will also vary for the same item, sold by different companies, but price alone may not be the ultimate consideration. You will have to take into account the quality, the quantity, and the service connected with that price. These things you will learn for yourself after you have dealt with a few of these concerns.

All of those listed have one common denominator: they will be fair and honest in their dealings with you. By that I do not mean they are incapable of making mistakes. We all do that. If, however, such a case occurs, your wisest course is to call the error to their attention immediately, so that it can be rectified. Unless you return unwanted goods, or point out a discrepancy in the charge, you will both have lost, since you will have become a disappointed customer for no good reason, and the supplier will have lost one, never knowing why. A mail-order house depends on, above all else, a good reputation.

Since most of the mail-order houses are likely to be some distance from you, it is difficult to be able to go there in person to select your material, which is the ideal way to purchase these items. However, if you are close enough, or will be traveling in their region, it would pay you to give one of them a call and make an appointment to come over. Telephone first because they are mail-order houses and will in all likelihood be busy enough trying to expedite their orders to those tiers who, having ordered by mail, deserve the courtesy of receiving their merchandise as soon as possible.

If, during the winter months, when the tying season is at its height, a number of tiers decided to meander into one of their favorite mail-order companies, there would be a certain amount of confusion since only a few employees may be able to serve them. In addition, it would also create a backlog on the outgoing mail orders, a situation the owners of these companies try to prevent.

January, February, and especially March are the busiest months for any company dealing in fly-tying materials. March, for the tier and fisherman, is like Christmas to a child. The season's opener is drawing near, and there is a sudden realization that a certain number of patterns have not been tied and to go astream without them would be a disaster. Thus, like the last-minute holiday shopper, who has forgotten Aunt Sarah and Cousin Luke, the tier runs about, as it were, and mills with the crowd trying to squeeze in these belated details before the choir sings "Silent Night"—or, in his case, before the line forms along the banks of his favorite stream.

By the middle of March all tiers, that is, the tardy ones, have to have their materials *yesterday*. The professional tiers are as guilty as the rest of us, for though their supply may be larger, they will get last-minute orders for finished flies from sporting goods stores that have suddenly realized spring is nigh, and it's time to push the fishing, and drop the Ping-Pong and bowling.

March is both the best and the worst time to buy fly-tying materials. It's best because most of the feather and fur supplies are at their primest and newest, and the pickings are generally of a higher level than, say, in October or November. It is the worst because there is generally a longer wait, a rush, which in turn forms a cycle causing holes in some of the inventory; this results in a few "Out of Stock" quotes from the company.

If every tier could decide upon his needs well in advance, and have the patience to wait in the case of special grades and shades of materials, he would do better in the long run.

Local sporting goods stores often carry a certain stock of fly-tying materials; these are usually purchased from the larger mail-order houses, and in some cases, direct from wholesalers. Though the selection may not be as encompassing as that in the larger mail-order concerns, there is an advantage of being able to pick and choose to your individual taste, in addition to being served in person by a knowledgeable retailer.

Following is a partial listing of mail-order houses dealing in fly-tying materials. Many of them will also catalog related items such as rod-building components, fly-fishing equipment, flies, and so on.

Angler's Roost
141 East 44th Street
New York, N.Y. 10017

Dan Bailey's Fly Shop
Livingston, Montana 59047

Bodmer's Fly Shop
2404 East Boulder Street
Colorado Springs, Colorado 80909

Buz's Fly and Tackle Shop
805 West Tulare Avenue
Visalia, California 93277

Harry and Elsie Darbee
Livingston Manor, New York 12758

Fireside Angler
Box 823
Melville, New York 11746

Fly Fisherman's Bookcase Tackle
  Service
138 Grand Street
Croton-on-Hudson, New York 10520

Herter's, Inc.
Rural Route 1
Waseca, Minnesota 56093

E. Hille
815 Railway Street
Williamsport, Pennsylvania 17701

Jack's Tackle
301 Bridge Street
Phoenixville, Pennsylvania 19460

Bud Lilly's Fly Shop
West Yellowstone, Montana 59758

The Orvis Company
Manchester, Vermont 05254

Rangeley Region Sports Shop
Rangeley, Maine 04970

Reed Tackle
Box 390
Caldwell, New Jersey 07006

S & M Fly Tying Materials
95 Union Street
Bristol, Connecticut 06010

Robert J. Stone
20 Brookside Circle
Springfield, Massachusetts 01129

E. Veniard, Ltd.
138 Northwood Road
Thornton Heath, Surrey, England

14 Conservation, Importation, and Federal Regulations

To "conserve" is "to keep from loss, decay and waste; to protect, supervise, to preserve." As a fisherman and a sportsman you are by nature a conservationist, simply because you will always want fish to be in existence so that you can fish. As a hunter, your dollar, paid in the form of license fees, goes toward replenishing the stock of game in the fields. I doubt if one of us wants to see the source of his enjoyment taken away, and it is for this reason that there is an abundance of fish and game left for this and other generations to come. Were it not for the hunter and fisherman, there would not be nearly the amount and variety of wildlife still abundant in our land.

Conservation, however, extends beyond the fish we fish for and the game we hunt. It not only includes the preservation of all species of animals and fish, but all forms of life, from the tiniest insect to the tallest redwood. And though we may not have direct control, it should concern us when a species indigenous to some foreign country faces extinction.

If nature had been left alone, she would not be having all the trouble she has now, trying to keep her balance; but since man has upset this balance to an extreme degree, it becomes his responsibility to keep the scales as even as possible.

The federal and state governments have passed many laws against the misuse of our natural resources. This is good. They have not, however, passed any laws *for* the avoidance of loss, decay, or waste. This is sad. It is also *not* true conservation.

Laws that have been passed by the federal and state legislatures were designed to protect the various forms of wildlife, and in so doing they have left no room for exceptions. The only exceptions I am searching for are the ones that would allow the use of feathers, furs, or what have you, of animals that have already died, whether through accident or old age. To allow this possible source of "use" to suffer loss through decay is waste, or, in the dictionary definition, the opposite of "conservation."

The argument you and I will get from the legislators is that, if exceptions were made, they would then unlawfully be taken advantage of. Do laws against theft eliminate thieves? Those who would take advantage will do so, whether there are laws or not. The true sportsman and conservationist does not need a law to tell him what is right or wrong. He will in most cases lend his aid in this direction, far beyond that which is required.

What am I getting at? In most of the previous chapters of this work I have been trying to impart the idea of searching for new horizons in the field of fly tying, especially by using certain parts of birds and animals you may not have thought of using. Everything has its use and purpose. All you have to do is find it. Don't waste it.

You may ask: "If such is the case, what can be done about it?" Have the laws changed. Now it is your turn to crusade. Incidentally, there are many people in the department of Fish and Wildlife who will agree with you that to waste anything is wrong, but they are bound to uphold the law.

IMPORTATION

Directly connected with conservation is the matter of importation of feathers and bird skins. Though I have advised you that the matter of importation of various materials is, for the individual, more bother than it is worth and should be left to the larger supply houses, you will, if you pursue this course, have to follow certain regulations. These regulations are set forth by the United States Department of Interior, Fish and Wildlife Division, and enforced by the Department of Customs.

The importation of any feather or bird skin, of any species that is considered wild, whether game bird or pest variety, is prohibited. To this rule there are a few exceptions, one of them being the ringneck pheasant.

The other exceptions are certain pheasants, namely the golden, Lady Amherst, Reeves, and silver. Also included in the exceptions is the mandarin wood duck.

To import these last-mentioned feathers or skins, you must apply for a permit from the Bureau of Fisheries and Wildlife. These particular species are importable under a quota system. For complete information write to:

United States Department of Interior
Fish and Wildlife Service
Bureau of Sport Fisheries and Wildlife
Washington, D.C. 20025

The fee for importing under the quota system is ten dollars, if your permit is granted. Applicants for annual quotas are required to submit their applications each June. If the annual quota for a certain species has not been filled, you may apply for a reallocation quota in September. You will have to state the firm you are purchasing the feathers from, the amount, and the purpose you intend to use the feathers for.

If you are interested in learning more about the rules and regulations in complete detail, write to:

United States Government Printing Office
Superintendent of Documents
Washington, D.C. 20042

and ask them to send you a copy of a book entitled *Code of Federal Regulations —Title 50—Wildlife and Fisheries.* This book costs $1.25.

For the importation of rooster or hen necks, or any feather that comes from a domestic fowl of a foreign country, no license is required to import, unless you order in excess of two hundred and fifty dollars' worth. After that amount you would need a license to import, or employ a broker who is licensed to clear the shipment for you once it arrives at your home port of entry.

Whether of domestic stock, or feathers coming in under the special quota system, all merchandise will have to be affirmed as to country of origin. If, for example, you are ordering rooster necks from India, you will have to get your exporter to have his invoice documented by an official of the Indian government, that the necks in question are indeed of "Domestic Indian Origin."

All feathers *that are on the skin of the bird,* whether a large silver pheasant or a small rooster neck, will have to be routed through the United States Department of Agriculture, after they have cleared Customs. After the USDA has affixed its seal upon your package it must then be sent to an authorized decontamination center for fumigation against possible infectious virus. Most of the mail-order houses that supply you are equipped to do this service for you at a fixed fee. It's fixed best, however, if you ask them first if they will undertake this process; their answer will depend on how busy they are. When you have found someone who will decontaminate your necks, you must advise the Department of Agriculture to send your materials to that particular company. This should be done in writing.

The USDA will keep any shipment from entering the country if the species of bird, or skin, has any bone in or on it. In the case of complete golden pheasant heads, having the tippets and the crest, it will be required that the bony beak of the bird first be severed from the cape before clearance is allowed. In such instances it would be more convenient to have your exporter do it for you, so that you will not come face to face with that problem and have your shipment delayed.

Upon arrival, and after having cleared the necessary red tape, your package will come to you with a customs slip attached, and you will be required to pay the duty due on the contents to the postal official or mailman you have received it from. In cases where your shipment has had to go to a decontamination center, the duty will be paid by those companies and you will have to reimburse them.

If you should send for a catalog from one of the English firms, such as E. Veniard, Ltd., you will notice that they have for sale a very complete line of fly-tying materials, especially in the feather section. This catalog will state that certain of their materials are not available to you as a United States customer, because of our laws. This is true. In that country certain game birds, legally shot, may be sold for the purpose of fly tying. This is a wise use of a natural resource, and no waste ensues. Do not, however, try to smuggle into the United States any of these prohibited birds or their feathers. They may simply only be confiscated, and you'll have lost your money, or worse, you may have rendered yourself *liable to a criminal charge*. It simply is not worth the risk involved.

Perhaps one day we will have regulations that will allow legitimately taken game, or pest birds, to enter this country for the use of our fly-tying needs. This is something we will all have to work at.

Besides covering the importation of wild and domestic bird skins, the Department of Interior also controls all migratory wildlife in this country. Check these, and also your home state regulations.

State laws can be checked by writing to your conservation department. These will control the kinds of birds and animals that may be taken during hunting season, the pest varieties, and the protection of various songbirds. They will also state the legality of possession of certain species.

With all the rules and regulations pertaining to wildlife, it makes us wonder if their use in fly tying is worth the trouble. Don't worry. *There must be deliberate intent to break these regulations in order for you to be liable.* As a flyfisherman, you can be assured that you have done more than your share, and will continue to do so, in the matter of conservation.

Selected Bibliography

The works listed have been helpful to me in compiling this book. For your interest you may wish to look into a few of them.

Austin, Oliver L., Jr. *Birds of the World*. New York: Golden Press, 1961.

Bates, Joseph D., Jr. *Streamer Fly Tying and Fishing*. Harrisburg, Pa.: The Stackpole Company, 1950, 1966.

Cahalane, Victor H. *Mammals of North America*. New York: The Macmillan Company, 1961.

Collins, Henry Hill, Sr. *Field Guide to American Wildlife*. New York: Harper & Row, 1959.

Flick, Art. *New Streamside Guide to Naturals and Their Imitations*. New York: Crown Publishers, Inc., 1969.

Lawrie, W. H. *All Fur Flies and How to Dress Them*. Cranbury, N.J.: A. S. Barnes & Co., 1967.

Leisenring, James E., and Hidy, Vernon S. *The Art of Tying the Wet Fly & Fishing the Flymph*. New York: Crown Publishers, Inc., 1971.

O'Connor, Jack, and Goodwin, George G. *The Big Game Animals of North America*. New York: Outdoor Life—E. P. Dutton & Co., Inc., 1961, 1964.

Robbins, Chandler S.; Bruun, Bertel; and Zim, Herbert S. *Birds of North America*. New York: Golden Press, 1966.

Roseborough, E. H. (Polly). *Tying and Fishing the Fuzzy Nymphs*. Manchester, Vt.: The Orvis Company, 1969.

Swisher, Doug, and Richards, Carl. *Selective Trout*. New York: Crown Publishers, Inc., 1971.

Index